NETWORK MARKETING MADE SIMPLE

A GUIDE FOR TRAINING NEW DISTRIBUTORS

DAVID M. WARD

GOLDEN LANTERN BOOKS

CONTENTS

YOUR FREE GIFT

INTRODUCTION

THE TRUTH ABOUT TRAINING NEW DISTRIBUTORS

The best way to train new network marketing distributors is to get them doing the activities as quickly as possible.

They need to get on the phone or out in the field talking to people. They need to recruit and make money.

Doing the activities is the best way to build their belief in the business and in themselves, and the best way for them to learn the business.

Yes, they should go to the company or team training or watch the training videos. New distributors need to learn about your company and products and how to recruit and sell. But they don't need to know everything. Not yet anyway.

For now, they need to know how to get started. They can learn the rest as they go along.

In fact, too much training or information can be overwhelming. Many new distributors spend too much time reading and thinking and never get around to *doing*. Too much information often leads to "paralysis of analysis".

Get your new distributors enough information to get them started and get them out in the field.

One way to do that is to use this book.

Network Marketing Made Simple provides the basic information every new distributor needs. It shows them how to start their business, how to recruit and make money, and how to get to the next level.

It's not meant to replace your company or team training, but to support it. By reading this book first, new distributors will be better prepared to absorb the information in your company or team training and more likely to follow the system they are taught.

Network Marketing Made Simple is divided into 3 parts:

GETTING STARTED

PART 1 is about the basics of network marketing. It teaches new distributors what they need to know and do to get their business off to a good start.

GETTING YOUR FIRST DISTRIBUTOR

PART 2 shows them how to recruit their first distributor. It teaches them how to identify and approach prospects, how to show them information about your products or services and your business opportunity, and how to determine if their prospects are ready to take the next step.

GETTING TO THE NEXT LEVEL

PART 3 shows distributors how to find and recruit more prospects, and *better* prospects. They'll learn how to use events for recruiting and training, and how to become a leader and help their organization grow.

WHAT YOU WILL LEARN

In *Network Marketing Made Simple,* your new distributors (or *you* if you are a new distributor) will learn:

- Why you should LAUNCH your new business, not just start it. . .and how to do it right

- 3 steps to recruiting your first distributor (and your second, third, fourth. . .)

- The best ways to approach prospects and get them to look at your business and products

- How to recruit more distributors in less time

- How to do an effective game plan with new distributors

- 3 types of "exposures" (and 3 ways to do them)

- The no-pressure way to close prospects and get them signed up

- Basic leadership skills for building your team

- And much more

WHO AM I?

My name is David Ward and I live in southern California. I was a practicing attorney for more than twenty years before I started my network marketing business. My law practice was successful, but I was always working and didn't have time for much else. I started a network marketing business to build passive income so I could reduce my work hours (and stress level!) and eventually retire.

And that's exactly what I did.

I started my business part-time, a few hours a week. It wasn't easy. No business is. But within a few years, I had built a six-figure passive income in my network marketing business and retired from practicing law.

I was finally able to do some of the things I had always wanted to do, including writing, and have written several books on network marketing.

3 THINGS YOU NEED TO KNOW

The idea for this book came from a live training I did for new distributors and their uplines. I wanted to present an overview of what we do in network marketing in a way that was easy to understand, easy to remember, and most importantly, easy to do. I came up with the idea of limiting each topic to just 3 ideas.

Each of my slides had a title and 3 bullet points—3 words or phrases relating to the subject. My first slide, for example, said, "3 OBJECTIVES FOR TONIGHT," followed by 3 words that described these objectives:

1) INFORM

2) INSPIRE

3) INOCULATE

I explained that my first objective was to **INFORM** them about the basics of network marketing and show them how to get their business started.

My second objective, I said, was to **INSPIRE** them about what's possible in this business, so they would get excited and be eager to begin.

My third objective was to **INOCULATE** them, meaning I wanted to protect them by showing them how to avoid some of the mistakes often made by new distributors.

My "3 Things" training was a hit. The new distributors told me they understood what they needed to do in the business and they were excited to get started. The experienced distributors were also excited, they told me, because it provided a simple way to get their new distributors quickly up to speed and taking action.

This book is structured the same way as that training. Each chapter begins with 3 words or phrases, followed by a brief explanation of the 3 topics related to that chapter. The chapters are short and can read and digested in a few minutes.

Each chapter ends with **"ACTION STEPS/POINTS TO REMEMBER"** that help the reader remember the most important points and understand what to do next.

HOW TO USE THIS BOOK

There are several ways you can use this book:

1) If you have a new distributor

Ask your new distributors to get a copy of this book. You might buy them a copy as a "welcome gift".

When I recruit a new distributor, *this* is the book I want them to read. My other network marketing books provide more detailed information, but they aren't ready for that. I want them to get started and get some results, first. Then they will be ready to learn more.

Ask your new distributors to read **PART 1** and call you when they are done. They will have questions for you to answer and you can point them to additional resources or training.

When they're ready, do the same thing with **PART 2** and **PART 3**.

2) If you are a new distributor

If you are a new distributor, start by reading **PART 1** and doing the *action steps* at the end of the chapters. Ask your sponsor or upline leader for additional information specific to your company, team, products, or systems. Ask them to do a "game plan" with you and help you launch your business.

When you're ready, go to **PART 2** and start recruiting.

3) **If you have a team**

If you already have distributors on your team, read the entire book, but especially **PART 3**. Think about how you can use this information to work with your team.

You can also use this as a workbook or "teacher's guide" for training your team in a group setting, either from the front of the room or on conference calls.

On a weekly conference call, for example, you can assign each distributor one or more chapters to read and summarize for the rest of the group. Or you can have everyone read the same chapter(s) and share their thoughts and their plans for the upcoming week.

4) **Other uses**

If you are thinking about starting a network marketing business, this will give you a clear picture of what you will be doing when you start. You can also ask potential sponsors what kind of training and support is provided by their company and see how it compares with the information in this book.

If you are speaking to a prospect who wants to know how network marketing works, you can have them read this book or you can use the information to answer their questions.

You can also use this book as a refresher course, or to better understand something you learned at your company or team training.

NETWORK MARKETING REALLY IS SIMPLE

Network marketing isn't brain surgery. You can learn the basics in a few hours and the basics are **eighty percent** of the business.

They're also easy to learn and easy to do.

They're called *basics* because everyone can do them. That's the magic of the network marketing business model. You can do them and your team can do them. The only question is will you?

Jim Rohn says, "What's easy to do is also easy to *not* do." It's easy to do the things you are about to learn. It's also easy to say, "I'm tired," or "I'm busy," and put them off for another day.

That's what many people do. And that's why many people fail.

If you want to succeed in network marketing, you need to learn the basics, do them consistently, and teach them to your team.

Let's get started.

PART I

GETTING STARTED

If you're like most people who start a network marketing business, you are experiencing two very different emotions.

First, you are excited. You know you are beginning something that could dramatically change your life and you can't wait to get started.

The second emotion you may be feeling is fear. When you think about actually doing the activities—talking to people, showing them your products or services, asking if they are interested—your heart beats faster, your mouth gets a little dry, and you wonder what you've gotten yourself into.

These emotions are normal. Most people feel them to some extent. And they're not a bad thing.

Your excitement will get you out of bed in the morning, eager to start the day. Your fears will help you to treat your business like a business and you will get better results.

In **PART 1** of this book is all about getting started. You'll learn some of the basic ideas you need to know, and some of the basic activities you need to do, to get your business off to a good start. As you learn these things, you will probably find that you are even more excited and less fearful because you'll see that this is really something you can do.

So get excited and stay excited!

START WITH EASY

The most important part of starting a new business is getting started, and the key to getting started is to do easy things first. Mark Twain put it this way:

"The secret of getting ahead is getting started. The secret of getting started is breaking your complex overwhelming tasks into small manageable tasks, and then starting on the first one."

Facebook's Mark Zuckerberg said, "I think a simple rule of business is, if you do the things that are easier first, then you can actually make a lot of progress."

Zuckerberg started Facebook as a little dorm room project. It was easy for him, and fun. He didn't think about everything he might have to do if his project took off. He just started and one thing led to another.

You can do the same.

Don't try to figure everything. Don't get try to learn everything, or worry about what happens next.

Just start. Start with easy.

3 THINGS YOU NEED TO KNOW

1. THIS IS A BUSINESS

2. IT TAKES TIME

3. YOU HAVE HELP

There are 3 philosophies about network marketing you need to know.

1. THIS IS A BUSINESS

If you started your business because you want to earn some "extra income," you can do that, and you probably won't need to put in a lot of time or effort.

If you want to earn a lot of income, however, you need to treat your business like a real business.

Not a hobby. Not a lottery ticket. Not something you "try" for thirty days or ninety days, but a real business that could eventually earn you a full time income.

Because it can.

If you treat your business like a hobby, it will cost you like a hobby. If you treat it like a business, it will pay you like a business.

Many distributors say they want to earn big money in their business, but they don't treat it like a real business. They don't go to the training or other events, or they only go once or twice and think they know everything there is to know. They don't do the activities consistently, they do them when they "find" extra time.

One reason many distributors aren't serious about their business they were able to start the business for very little money. They invested $25, $100, or $500 and if they lose that, it's not the end of the world.

So they don't commit to the business. They don't treat their business like a real business.

If you want to earn significant income in your business, imagine you had invested $250,000 to start your business instead of a few hundred dollars. Would your attitude towards the business be different?

Of course it would.

You would show up every day, ready to work. You would take every opportunity to learn the business and work hard to make your business a success. You would treat your business like a real business because you wouldn't want to lose your $250,000 investment.

If you want to earn a significant income in your business, you must treat it like a real business. If you do, you could earn a lot more than many people who invest $250,000 in a traditional business.

2. IT TAKES TIME

You can earn money in network marketing fairly quickly. Many people do. But the big money and best results probably won't happen overnight.

Your first year in the business, everything is new. Most people take awhile to get good at the business.

In the beginning, you'll get some sales and earn some money, but not that much at first. That's okay. You're new. Give it time.

You'll sign up some distributors. Some will do a lot, some will do a little, and some will do nothing.

That's okay. That's normal. Keep going, and give it time.

Keep recruiting and you will find some leaders, distributors who are serious about the business. They will recruit distributors and find leaders, and your organization will grow.

Stick with it. As more people join your organization and those people bring in more people, your business will start growing faster and faster.

In the beginning it's just you. Eventually there are ten of you working the business. Ten will grow to 100, and eventually, you'll have 1,000 in your organization, contributing to your income.

Eventually, you will hit the tipping point in your business and your organization and your income will experience rapid growth. You may have months where you income doubles or *triples*.

That's the way it works, if you give it time and continue to do the work.

In the beginning, you work hard and have small results. A few years from now, you could be earning an amazing income without having to do much work at all.

You can become rich in network marketing, if that's what you want to do, but it's going to take time.

Don't judge your business by what happens your first few months, or even your first year. Keep working. Keep recruiting. Keep building your business.

Good things await you, but only if you give it time.

3. YOU HAVE HELP

You're in business for yourself, but not BY yourself. You have lots of help.

You have the support of your company, which provides the products or services, creates the marketing materials and websites, hires and trains the home office employees, and pays the distributors.

If customers have questions, they can call and speak with customer service. If distributors have questions or want to order more brochures or DVDs, they can call the company.

The company does all of this, and more, so that you are free to build your business. You do the marketing, the company does nearly everything else.

You also have a support team of upline distributors who want you to be successful. They train you. They do presentations for your prospects and help you sign them up. They conduct training and leadership calls for you and your team, and they do all of this because the company pays them a percentage of all of the business written by you and your organization.

You also have help from your organization—the distributors you recruit and the distributors they recruit. As the individuals in your organization build their businesses, you earn overrides on their volume. By building their business, they help your business grow.

You also have help from distributors who are sideline to you (neither above nor below you). They will help you and your team because they know that you will help them and their team. You can introduce them to your prospects at the events or on the phone. They'll share their story and encourage your prospects to sign up.

You're in business for yourself, but not by yourself.

ACTION STEPS/POINTS TO REMEMBER

- Make a commitment to treat your business like a business. Schedule regular time for your business activities. Focus on doing the activities, not your short term results, and give your business time to grow.

- Find out the names and contact information of your upline leaders. Introduce yourself to them (or ask your sponsor to introduce you). Tell them you're looking forward to working with them.

- Go through the company website and note the resources that are available to you. Spend 15 minutes per day exploring these resources.

3 THINGS YOU NEED TO HAVE

1. DESIRE

2. WILLINGNESS TO LISTEN

3. WILLINGNESS TO WORK

Success in network marketing doesn't require a lot of talent, time, or money. Here are three things it does require:

1. DESIRE

The number one key to success in *any* business is a strong desire to succeed.

When you have a burning desire to succeed, you'll do whatever it takes to make it. If there are obstacles, you'll overcome them. If you have bad days, you'll push through them. If things seem difficult, you'll figure them out.

When your desire is strong, you keep going because you know that it's worth it.

In *Think and Grow Rich*, Napoleon Hill said, "The starting point of all achievement is desire. Keep this constantly in mind. Weak desires bring weak results, just as a small fire makes a small amount of heat."

Think about what you want to accomplish in your business. You may say that you started your business to earn more income, and while that may be true, there is also a deeper reason. *Why* do you want to earn more income? What will you do with the money? Why is *that* important to you?

If you want to pay off some credit card debt, how will you feel when you do? That feeling is your "why".

The stronger your why, the more you will be motivated to succeed.

The best "why" has an emotional element to it. The thought of not having it may bring you close to tears.

Perhaps you started your business because you are frustrated with coming home late at night after your kids are asleep. You want to have more time with them. This is important to you. If you are struggling in your business and feel like quitting, reminding yourself that you're doing the business so you can have more time with your kids will keep you going.

Your why may be something you *don't* want: "I'm in this business because I never want to work for someone else again," or, "I'm doing this so I will never again have to tell my wife we can't afford the vacation I promised her."

When you have a strong why—a burning desire to succeed in this business—you won't let anything, or anyone, stop you.

So, why did you start your business? What is your why?

Share your why with your spouse. They need to know what you're working towards, and why it is important to you. They need to understand why you're working extra hours, or why you're spending money on a business that isn't yet producing much income.

You might also share your why with your sponsor, upline, or

workout partner. When you're having a bad day, encourage them to remind you of your why.

2. WILLINGNESS TO LISTEN

Success in network marketing isn't about only what you do. It's about learning a simple system (simple, meaning something anyone can do), following that system, and helping your new distributors do the same.

Systems mean everyone does things essentially the same way, using the same tools and approaches and methods that everyone else uses.

Some distributors refuse to follow that system. They insist on doing things their own way. They may have some personal success doing that, but they will never grow a big team.

Why? Because network marketing isn't about any one of us, it's about a large group of people. Each distributor may only do a little, but it adds up to a lot, and you get a percentage.

Therefore, success in network marketing is about doing things that duplicate.

You learn the system, you follow it (do the activities), you help your team do it, they help their team do it, and so on. When everyone follows the same system, the organization duplicates and grows. If everyone uses a different system, however, it leads to confusion.

You may have some great ideas for building your business. Put them away for now and follow the system used by your upline leaders. That system worked for them and for many other distributors, and it will work for you.

Follow that system even if you don't agree with everything. Later, when you are successful and know the system inside and out, you might introduce a new idea or a new method. But not now.

Learn the rules before you break the rules. Follow the system before you attempt to change it.

3. WILLINGNESS TO WORK

You may have a burning desire, you may be willing to listen and follow the system used by your upline, but to succeed, you must also be willing to do the work.

Many people get started in network marketing with unreasonable expectations. They think it will be easy to build their business. They think they just need to sign up a few people and those people will build the business and make them rich.

That's silly. Nobody is going to build your business for you. You have to build it yourself.

You must do the activities. You have to talk to people, send them information, and follow up. You have to help them get started and trained and you have to be there to support them and help them get their business going.

They will build their business, not yours. But because they are in your organization, as their business grows, so will yours.

But only if you do the work.

ACTION STEPS/POINTS TO REMEMBER

- Think about your "why". Write it down and refer to it often. Share it with your spouse and your sponsor and ask them to hold you accountable.

- Commit to following the system taught to you by your upline support team. Put your "new ideas" away for now.

- Make the decision that you will do the work, no matter what. Tell yourself, "It may be hard, but it's worth it".

3 THINGS WE DO

1. RETAIL AND RECRUIT

2. WORK WITH OUR TEAM

3. PERSONAL DEVELOPMENT

In network marketing, there are 3 key activities we do to earn money and build our business:

1. RETAIL AND RECRUIT

We earn commissions when we sell something to a retail customer or to our personally sponsored distributors. We earn overrides when someone on our team sells something.

Overrides are passive income. Someone in your organization sells something and you get paid a percentage.

Residual income comes from renewals or re-orders. The sale was made once by you or someone on your team. When a customer (retail or wholesale/distributor) re-orders or renews, you get paid again.

As your team recruits more distributors, your passive and residual incomes grow. At some point, you may retire or slow down in building your business, but as long as your organization continues to retail and recruit, you will continue to earn overrides. As long as customers renew or re-order, you will continue to receive residual income.

(Note, your company's comp plan may require you to meet certain qualifications to earn overrides and residual income.)

In the beginning, 100% of your income will come from your own efforts. As you recruit others, and they do the same, your override income will grow. As your team volume grows, eventually, most (or all) of your income will come from overrides and renewals.

Network marketing is based on leverage. Instead of one person (you) generating all of the sales volume in your business, that volume comes from the collective efforts of a lot of people in your organization. Each distributor might do a little, but that can add up to a lot, and you earn overrides and residual income on those sales.

In network marketing, recruiting is king. It gives you maximum leverage. You may earn a lot of money through retailing products or services, but you can earn *more* through recruiting. No matter how much you can do yourself, a team of people can do more.

2. WORK WITH OUR TEAM

The second thing we do in network marketing is work with our team. When you're new, you work with your upline "support" team, i.e., your sponsor and other distributors above you in the genealogy. They will help you get your business started, answer questions, and show you how to retail and recruit.

Your upline will also help you with your prospects. They will speak to them, either in person or via a 3-way call, answer their questions, invite them to events, and "close" them (help them decide to sign up). They will also help you get them trained. Working with your upline is how you learn the business.

You watch your upline and other distributors do the activities so you can see how they're done. You might go with them on appointments and watch what they do with their prospects. They might come with you to see *your* prospects. You simply introduce them and then watch what they do.

You also watch them speak to their own prospects and with their other distributors. They do it, you watch. You do it, and they watch you, and show you how to improve.

As you gain experience, you will start working the distributors in your organization. Your upline will continue to help you with some of these tasks, but eventually, they will do less and you will do more.

You'll help your team get started, teach them the basics, and assist them with their prospects. Eventually, your team will do most of these things for their organization.

3. PERSONAL DEVELOPMENT

The third thing we do in network marketing is work on ourselves. Jim Rohn said, "Work harder on yourself than on your business," and we do because to a great extent, we *are* our business.

We improve our skills by attending trainings, reading books, watching videos, and listening to audios. We watch how successful distributors do the business. We seek their advice, listen to them on the phone, watch them do presentations, and watch them speaking with their team.

We learn about our products or services. We learn how to talk to prospects and with our team.

The more we work on ourselves, the better we get at doing the activities. We're able to do them faster and get better results. As we work with our team, we become leaders and learn how to inspire people to a better future.

Go to every training, even if you've been to the same training before. The information may be the same, but you will be different.

The first time you hear the information, everything is new. You then apply the information and get some results, and see how that information is applied in the real world. The next time you hear that training, you will have a different context because you have actually used the information.

ACTION STEPS/POINTS TO REMEMBER

- Ask your upline to explain your comp plan, or show you where to get the details. Find out how much you earn in commissions and overrides at different levels, and what you need to do to reach those levels. Find out if there are any bonuses and what you have to do to earn them. Ask if there are qualifications you need to meet to receive overrides and residual income.

- As you work with your upline, ask lots of questions and take lots of notes. Make sure you understand the system used by your company or team. Commit to using that system and helping your team to do the same.

- Schedule 30 minutes a day for personal development. Ask your upline for a list of recommend books. Get a work out partner and help each other practice the activities.

3 KEYS TO GETTING STARTED RIGHT

1. FOCUS

2. RESPONSIBILITY

3. CONSISTENCY

Here are 3 keys to starting right in your new business.

1. FOCUS

If you were opening a restaurant, you wouldn't also open a shoe store or flower shop. It's difficult enough to build one business, let along two completely different businesses at the same time.

We've all heard about the value of "multiple streams of income". Mark Twain had a different view. He said, "Put all your eggs in one basket. . .and watch that basket".

Focus is achieved by adopting an attitude that says, "I'm making this a priority in my life. I'm putting aside other things so I will have the time and energy to do this to the best of my ability."

Focus means making a commitment to excellence in your business, and being willing to make sacrifices in order to achieve superior results.

Richard Koch, author of *The 80/20 Principle*, recommends that we, "Strive for excellence in a few things, rather than good performance in many".

That's focus.

Focus means learning all you can about your company, your products, and about network marketing. It means cutting down on TV time, sports, hobbies, and other activities that don't serve you in your quest to build a business and achieve your most important goals.

You may only have a few hours a week for your business, and that's fine. But this means you have to be even more focused than you might be if you had the whole day.

When you are working your business, you must eliminate distractions. If you're making calls, turn off social media and don't check email until later in the day. Close your door and tell your family you are working and that if they want to talk to you they need to wait until you are done.

Make your business a priority. Focus on it. Give it as much time and energy as possible.

2. RESPONSIBILITY

This is *your* business. You are responsible for everything that happens.

You have help, but don't wait for anybody to do anything, and don't blame anybody if they don't.

If there are problems, fix them. If you don't know how to do something, look it up or ask someone to point you in the right direction.

Your sponsor and upline have a financial incentive to help you, but don't depend on them. If they do help you, be appreciative, but don't assume that it will continue.

Your sponsor isn't going to build your business for you. They aren't going to put distributors under you, give you sales, or loan you money.

You are responsible for your business. If you fail, you have nobody to blame but yourself. If you succeed, you get the credit.

Yes, you will have help, but if you must take responsibility for your own business. When you accept that responsibility, you have the power to make your dreams come true.

You have the same company, the same products, and the same comp plan as every distributor in your company. The only variable is *you*. If someone else is having success in your company, you can, too. But it's up to you to make that happen because it's your business.

Hal Elrod said, "The moment you take responsibility for everything in your life, is the moment you can change anything in your life."

3. CONSISTENCY

Successful distributors are consistent. They work the business every day, five or six days a week. Unsuccessful distributors work the business when they can find the time.

Consistent daily activities is important because it's too easy to get distracted and miss a day. One day turns into two. Before you know it, you've done nothing this week. You think, "I'll get started again next week," but something else comes up. One week becomes two weeks and soon, you're not doing the business at all.

It's better to work the business daily because the work becomes a habit. You know what you're going to do each day and you do it. The more you do it, the better you get at it. The better you get, the better your results.

Daily activity allows you to build momentum. Because you're not stopping and starting all the time, one day builds upon the next. You get better and faster, and you start seeing more results, which motivates you to continue.

Consistency means being on all the training calls and at all the events. It means working your business like you would a job—showing up every day, doing the work, letting people see that they can count on you.

Consistency also means doing things the same way each time. Once you have found something that works for you—an approach, a method, a tool—stick with it. You may get bored doing it the same way, but as long as you are getting good results, don't change anything. Stay consistent and get more good results.

ACTION STEPS/POINTS TO REMEMBER

- Commit to making this business a top priority. Tell your family and your sponsor. Make a list of things you won't do, or will cut down on doing, to free up time for this business.

- Take responsibility for everything that happens in your business. Be proactive. Don't wait for things to happen, make them happen.

- As you learn more about the business, make a checklist of your daily activities and do them every day. Don't stop work for the day until you have done everything on your list.

3 THINGS YOU NEED TO DO FIRST

1. LIST

2. TOOLS

3. SCHEDULE

To get your business started, there are 3 things you need to do first.

1. LIST

Start making a list of your "warm market" contacts. Warm market simply means people you know. Everyone else is "cold market".

Later, you'll learn how to find prospects in the cold market. Starting with your warm markct gives you an instant list of people you can talk to. You don't have to spend money on advertising or leads or do anything else.

Start by going through the contacts in your phone. Write down the name and phone number of all of your contacts.

Go through your paper address book, or computer database. Go through the directories for your school, church, neighborhood, or associations you belong to. Go through your email inbox. Go through the parent lists for your kid's dance class, soccer league, or girl scouts.

If you or your spouse own a business, go through the lists of clients or customers, vendors, suppliers, and professional contacts, and add them to your list.

Use a "memory jogger" (a list of occupations, cities, relationships, etc.) to remember people you know who may not be in your phone or on a list. If a memory jogger isn't available, go through the phone book for ideas, (i.e., Letter "A"—"Who do you know who is an accountant/works for an accountant/uses an accountant?")

The bigger your list, the better, so don't leave anyone off of your list. Don't pre-judge *anyone*. It's impossible to know whether anyone will be interested or not, and even if they're not interested in joining your business, they might buy your products or services or give you referrals.

And, if someone isn't interested today, they might be interested six months from now, when their situation has changed, or when they see you doing well in the business.

2. TOOLS

In network marketing, we use tools to show people our business opportunity and our products or services. Tools include DVDs, websites, recorded messages, brochures, magazines and other printed material.

Find out which tools are available to you and review them. Talk to your sponsor and see which ones he or she uses. Order a supply of tools to hand out or show prospects, e.g., DVDs, brochures, flip chart. Consider ordering extras to give to your new distributors when they get started.

Sign up for the company website. Your sponsor should be able to help you do this and show you how to use it.

If you are in a product oriented business, order product samples, and/or inventory. And make sure you start using your products. Prospects will ask you how they have worked for you and you need to be able to tell them. Using your products or services will also build your belief in them and what they can do.

One of the most important tools you will need is 3-way calling on your phone. If you don't have it, order it. If you do have it, make sure you know how to use it.

You will use 3-way calling to introduce your prospects to other distributors who will answer their questions and help them decide to get started as a distributor. You will also use it to do "welcome calls" with your new distributors, to introduce them to your upline and other distributors.

3. SCHEDULE

Talk to your sponsor or upline and schedule your training class, if your company or team offers one. Find out if you need to register and do so. Put the training on your calendar and don't miss it. If there isn't a local training, find out what's available online.

In fact, don't talk to any prospects until you have gone through the training. This is important. You need to learn what to do when you approach people, and you want to do it the right way.

What should you say? What should you show them? What should you do if they ask questions?

You also need to know what NOT to do. You don't want your prospects to be confused or get the wrong impression about what you're offering them. You don't want to chase them away before they have seen the information. So. . .

Don't talk to anyone until you have been trained.

You should also schedule a "game plan" with your sponsor or upline. This is where you meet for an hour or two, set some goals for your business, and plan your launch or "grand opening".

Training is general information, for all distributors. Your game plan is specific to you. You'll learn about what happens at your game plan in the next chapter.

ACTION STEPS/POINTS TO REMEMBER

- Start your list. Shoot for at least 100 names in the next 48 hours. Keep adding names as you think of them. Don't pre-judge anyone or leave anyone off of your list.

- Order some tools. Order product samples and inventory. Make sure your phone has 3-way calling and that you know how to use it. Practice making a few 3-way calls with other distributors, before you do it with prospects. Ask your sponsor for names and phone numbers of distributors you can use to speak with your prospects.

- Contact your sponsor or upline and schedule your game plan and business launch.

3 THINGS TO DO AT YOUR GAME PLAN

1. GRADE YOUR LIST

2. ESTABLISH GOALS

3. PLAN THE LAUNCH

A "game plan" is a meeting with your sponsor or upline, to help you get your business started. They will help you establish a work schedule, tell you where and when local events take place, make sure you know about the tools that are available to you, and establish a simple plan to get your first sales and recruits.

Generally, there are 3 things that are covered during the game plan.

1. GRADE YOUR LIST

Your sponsor will go over your list with you, to make sure you have enough prospects to contact. If you haven't started your list, or you don't have enough names on it, they will help you start or expand your list.

Your sponsor will talk to you about the people on your list. They will ask about their background, how you know them, their personality, and if you know what they might want (e.g., more income, time freedom, etc.)

They may help you "grade" or prioritize your list, in terms of which prospects to approach first, the best ways to approach them, and/or which tools they recommend you use. This will also prepare them to help you speak with the people on your list.

Your sponsor may have you start contacting people during the game plan itself. You may call prospects and invite people to visit your website or listen to a recorded message, for example, or you may schedule an appointment to meet with them.

Your sponsor may coach you on what to say and how to say it, listen to you make a few calls and offer suggestions. Or they may ask you to introduce your prospects to them on the phone and listen to what they say to them, before having you make any calls on your own.

They may also have you send emails, texts, or put some tools (e.g., DVDs, magazines, etc.) in the regular mail.

2. GOALS

Your "why" is the big picture. Why are you doing this business? What do you want to achieve? Whom do you want to help?

During the game plan, your sponsor may ask you to establish some short term goals. You might want to write these down in advance and bring them to the game plan. Either way, you should share these goals with your sponsor. They need to know what you want to accomplish so they can help you make a plan to do that.

If you have a goal to earn a lot of money your first year, for example, your sponsor can make sure that you schedule enough activity to achieve that goal. If your short term goal is more modest, your sponsor needs to know that, too.

You might want to start with a ONE YEAR GOAL:

How much do you want to be earn your first year? Or how much do you want to be earning per month, 12 months from today?

You might also decide what level in the compensation plan you want to be at by the end of your first year.

Don't hesitate to think big. "If you limit your choices only to what seems possible or reasonable, you disconnect yourself from what you truly want, and all that is left is a compromise," said Robert Fritz.

You might also have a ONE MONTH GOAL:

How much would you like to earn during your first month? How much would get you excited? How much would prove to you that you are on the right path?

What would you do with the money? Paying bills is fine, but you might be more excited if you set a goal to buy yourself something you've been wanting for a long time, or that you can use in your new business.

How many distributors do you want to recruit your first month? What bonus or promotion do you want to achieve?

You can ask your sponsor "what's possible" but remember, these are your goals, and you might want to go for something bigger.

Choose goals that inspire you to take action.

3. LAUNCH

Many network marketing companies or teams recommend a "grand opening" event or events to launch a new distributor's business. The idea is to quickly get as many people as possible to see information about your new business and products or services.

You might launch your business with an in-home party ("showcase," "Private Business Reception" ("PBR")), where friends, family, and neighbors are invited to help you celebrate the start of your business and get information about your products and business opportunity.

You might launch your business by inviting people to a "Private Conference Call" ("PCC"), where they can hear this information presented by your sponsor or upline leader.

You might do a telephone blitz, where your sponsor or trainer helps you call people you know and invite them to see the information via a website or conference call, or schedule a time to meet with them.

Your launch event might involve mailing DVDs to people on your list, with a short note telling them you'll be contacting them to get their feedback.

If you own a business, you might do an event at your office, or schedule a series of Private Conference Calls for different groups of contacts, i.e., one call for clients or customers and another for your business contacts.

Your upline or sponsor will tell you which of these events or activities they recommend for your business launch, and help you plan and execute them.

ACTION STEPS/POINTS TO REMEMBER

- Keep working on your list before you meet your sponsor for your game plan.

- Set a one year goal and a one month goal and share your goals with your sponsor, so they can help you create your work schedule and establish some short term goals.

- Schedule your launch events to occur within your first week in the business.

3 TYPES OF STORIES YOU SHOULD KNOW

1. PRODUCT/SERVICE

2. BUSINESS

3. YOURS

In network marketing, the facts are important but it is often the stories that inspire people to act.

Facts tell, but stories sell.

Stories with people in them are effective because prospects can relate to those people, especially if they have something in common with them.

Stories don't have to be long or complicated. They can be as short as a single sentence. But every story has a beginning, a middle, and an end.

There are 3 types of stories you should know and use.

1. PRODUCT/SERVICE

As you learn more about your new business, pay attention to the stories you hear about people who have used your products or services and gotten good results. You'll want to share those stories with your prospects when you show them your products or services.

These stories are testimonials for your products. Being able to tell people what your products or services have done for real people is always better than telling them what your products are supposed to do.

You can learn stories by listening to online or local presentations, talking to other distributors, and reading through your company's brochures and website. As you develop a customer base, encourage them to share their stories with you.

You also want to use your company's products so that when a prospect asks, "How has it worked for you?" you will be able to tell them your own product success story.

Product stories follow a pattern. They all start with the customer's problem or need. That's followed by what they did about that problem, e.g., they bought your product. (They might first mention other solutions they tried that didn't work.)

The last part of the story is the result—how the product solved their problem and how they are today.

I used to have. . . Then I tried. . . Now I am. . .

Pay attention to the stories that are told about your products or services. Learn them and share them with your prospects and team.

2. BUSINESS

You should also learn stories about distributors who are having success building their business with your company. As you meet other distributors, ask them about their background, how they got started in the business, and how they are doing now.

Learn your upline's story and share that, too. Prospects will not only find out what's possible in the business, they will learn something about the people who will be helping them in the business.

If your upline has a big team, it means they've helped a lot of people become successful. Tell your prospects about what you upline has achieved. Your prospects will understand that if they were able to help others, they can help them, too.

Learn some stories about other distributors with your company who have different backgrounds. They don't need to be in your organization. You don't even have to know them personally to use their stories.

If one of your prospects is a real estate agent, for example, you'll want to tell them about another real estate agent who is having success with your company.

As you build your team, also share stories about the people in your organization. Your prospects (and new distributors) will want to know about the people you have worked with and helped.

3. YOUR STORY

The most important story to share is your own. Even if you're brand new, you have a story to tell and your prospects want to hear it.

Your story should include:

(1) Your background. What you do (i.e., your occupation) or what you did before becoming a distributor.

(2) Why you got started as a distributor. What you want to accomplish.

(3) What you accomplished so far, and/or what the business opportunity means to you (i.e., elaborate on what you want to accomplish, who you want to help, etc.)

If you have a product success story, you can incorporate that into your business story.

ACTION STEPS/POINTS TO REMEMBER

- Start collecting product stories. Listen, take notes, and learn them so you can share them with your prospects and team.

- Start collecting business success stories. Learn your upline's story and stories from distributors with different backgrounds. Start writing your own story.

- Practice telling these stories. Use them when you speak with your prospects. Remember, facts tell but stories sell.

3 WAYS WE SPEND OUR TIME

1. DAILY

2. WEEKLY

3. MONTHLY

As a new distributor, one of the first things you should do (and ask *your* new distributors to do) is to put your work schedule on your calendar. Start by calendaring regular events, such as your weekly business presentation, training, monthly event, convention. Then add your company and team calls and online events.

Next, schedule blocks of time for work activities, such as prospecting calls, follow-up calls, working with new distributors, and other money-generating activities. If you plan to work two hours a day during weekdays, you might consider one hour in the morning and one hour in the evening, to accommodate the work schedules and time zones of your prospects.

Think of the time you block out on your calendar as an appointment with yourself. Don't miss those appointments. If you have calendared 7:30 to 8:30 pm for your business, you should use that time for business and nothing else.

Here are some guidelines for making your schedule.

1. DAILY

Your top priority is *recruiting and retailing*. This is what generates income and builds your business.

Set aside time each work day (5 or 6 days per week) to contact *new* prospects and show them, or invite them to see, information about your business and/or your products or services. When they see this information, it is called an *exposure*.

Ask your upline how many daily exposures your team recommends. If they don't have a suggested amount, choose a number that you believe you can do consistently. If you do two or three exposures a day, you can make real progress in your business. Just make sure you do them every day.

You also need to schedule time each day to follow-up with prospects you have previously exposed. Make sure you schedule enough time to introduce your interested prospects to your upline or other distributors, via 3-way calls, to get their questioned answered and to help them sign up.

Finally, you should also schedule time each day for personal development. Schedule 20-30 minutes per day on your calendar for reading books and listening to audios. You can also listen to audios while you commute or exercise.

2. WEEKLY

Ask your sponsor or upline about the live events in your market and put these on your calendar. Also schedule weekly conference calls or online events hosted by your company or team. These might include training calls, team calls, leadership calls, and other types of calls or online "meetings".

When you schedule these events, allow enough time before they start for inviting prospects and your team. For example, if you have a local weekly business opportunity meeting every Tuesday night from 7-8 pm, allocate some time on Mondays and Tuesdays to invite guests (prospects) to the presentation, and remind your local team to do the same.

As your team grows, schedule some time each week for working with your team, especially your new distributors. You'll need time to do their game plan and launch events, and some time to help them get their new recruits started.

The amount of time will vary, depending on what training resources are available from your company or team, the amount of help available from your upline, and other factors.

3. MONTHLY

Many companies and teams have a regular monthly event, usually on a Saturday or Sunday. These events feature training and recognition of distributors' achievements, and often feature out-of-town guest trainers or corporate representatives. They may also include a business opportunity presentation for prospects.

The monthly event is a valuable tool for building your team. The larger crowds and special guest speakers, who usually have bigger income stories to tell, allow your team and prospects to see the big picture that awaits them with your company.

If there is a monthly event in your market, put the dates on your calendar. Schedule time during the month to promote each upcoming event to your team, and to invite guests to the business presentation.

Also set aside some time on the first or second day of each month to review your progress for the previous month and to set goals and plan your activities for the upcoming month.

ACTION STEPS/POINTS TO REMEMBER

- Schedule your daily, weekly, and monthly activities on your calendar. Ask your upline about annual conventions or leadership events and put these on your calendar, too. Start with regular events, then add your "work hours". Ask your sponsor about annual events like a convention or leadership retreat and put this on your calendar, too.

- Next, put your "work hours" on your calendar—for prospecting and follow-up calls and other income generating activities. Think about how you can also work your business at other times of the day. For example, you might make phone calls on your way to and from work. You can meet prospects on your lunch hour or coffee break. You can send emails or text while waiting at the doctor's office. And you can approach people you meet while you are out running errands. Always carry your calendar and a list of prospects with you so that when you have a few minutes free you can make some calls.

- Make sure your family knows about the time you have scheduled for your business. Ask them to respect this time and not disturb you until your work time is done for the day.

3 KEYS TO A FAST START

1. EXCITEMENT

2. URGENCY

3. BLINDERS

In starting your business, your objective is to quickly get some positive results. When you have some cash in your pocket and some distributors signed up, your belief in the business and your ability to succeed go way up.

Getting some results will also give you a story to share with your prospects. Your story tells them what's possible. If you can do it, they will know that they can do it, too.

Imagine being able to tell people, "I started my business last week, I've already earned $300 and have two new distributors in my organization, and I don't even know what I'm doing!"

That's the kind of story that gets people saying, "Tell me more!"

Here are 3 keys to a fast start in your business.

1. EXCITEMENT

The first key to a fast start is to get *excited*. When you are excited, it's easier to approach people because excitement is contagious. When you're excited, the people you talk to will be excited, and curious to know what's going on in your life.

Think about a time in your life when you started something new. Think about how you felt the day before your wedding, leaving for a big vacation, or starting a new job.

Think about your why. Think about your goals. Imagine yourself getting closer to achieving those goals.

You are starting a great journey, and that's exciting!

2. URGENCY

The second key to a fast start is having a sense of urgency about your business. If you want to make things happen quickly, RUN, don't walk. Don't wait until you're ready, do it now.

Talk to as many people as you can, as quickly as you can.

If someone can't look at the information immediately, ask if they can look at it this afternoon. If not this afternoon, how about tonight? Don't follow-up with someone in two weeks, follow-up in two days. Or two hours.

Urgency means communicating a message that says there's no time to waste. You want to talk to them now. They need to see the information now. You want to follow up with them immediately.

A sense of urgency tells people that what you are doing is important and can't wait. When they see you talk fast and move fast, they will be curious and want to know what "this" is all about.

Urgency also gives you posture. It tells people you know where you are going and you are going there with or without them. It says, "I'd love to work with you, but I don't need you to do this; take a look and let me know, but do it quickly because I've got to go."

And you really don't want to waste time with people who aren't interested. You want to move on and find people who are.

A sense of urgency will get more people looking at the information, and the more who look, the more will sign up.

3. BLINDERS

Some race horses are skittish. They get distracted and nervous seeing other horses running beside them and they pull up. To prevent this, their trainers put blinders on them, which prevent them from seeing what's next to them and can only see straight ahead.

That's what you need to do in this business.

If you want to be successful, you need to avoid looking at and listening to all of the distractions and noise around you.

And there is a lot of noise.

It may come from other distributors who don't follow the system and insist on telling you about some new method or tool they heard about and how it is the best way to go.

Don't listen to them. It's just noise. Stick with what successful distributors in your company are doing to build their business.

The noise may also come from well-meaning prospects, perhaps your family or friends, who might try to talk you out of what you're doing. They may say that network marketing doesn't work, that only a few people make any money, or that the whole industry is a scam.

Don't listen to them. It's just noise. Put your blinders on and run.

The noise may come from your own thoughts, as you have doubts about your ability, fears about being rejected, or other emotions. Thoughts like these are normal, but not to be taken seriously. Let them pass.

Put blinders on and run. Don't let anything distract you or slow you down. Don't get caught up in the paralysis of analysis that afflicts many distributors who are continually "getting ready" to start but never do.

Just start.

Don't worry about how it's all going to work out, just keep running and don't stop until you have crossed the finish line.

ACTION STEPS/POINTS TO REMEMBER

- Get excited! You are embarking on a life-changing journey.

- Have a sense of urgency in everything you do. In everything you do, move quickly. Don't delay. The business is much easier when you have a sense of urgency.

- Don't get distracted by anything around you or by your own thoughts. Don't wait until you know everything, get started and figure it out as you go along.

PART II

GETTING YOUR FIRST DISTRIBUTOR

There's nothing like getting your first check or direct deposit.

It's exciting!

It means the business really works. It means you did it.

That first check is important. From that day forward, nobody can tell you the business doesn't work. You have the check to prove that it does.

But as exciting as it is to get your first check, there is something that's even more exciting: getting your first *override*.

Getting an override means you are getting paid from the efforts of other people. It means you aren't merely exchanging your time for dollars, you own a real business.

Getting your first override starts with getting your first distributor. In **PART 2**, you'll learn how to do that. Once you recruit your first distributor, you'll know how to recruit your second distributor, and many more after that.

You'll also know how to help your distributor get *their* first distributor. And you'll be on your way.

If you're ready to get started, turn to the next chapter and learn the 3 steps to recruiting.

3 STEPS TO RECRUITING

1. APPROACH

2. EXPOSE

3. FOLLOW-UP & CLOSE

You've got your contact list. You've got some tools. You have 3-way calling enabled on your phone and a list of people you can call for help.

It's time to do some recruiting. Here are the 3 steps:

1. APPROACH

Recruiting starts with contacting the people on your list and either inviting them to look at some information, or asking them to look at that information as a favor to you.

The best way to contact people is over the phone. That way, you know you have their attention and you can get a commitment to meet with you or look at the information you send them.

You can use email or text to tell them you want to talk with them or meet with them, but it's best not to tell them anything about why you want to speak with them until you have their full attention.

When you speak to them, go to step 2 and show them the information.

You'll learn different approaches you can use in the next two chapters.

2. EXPOSE

After you have the prospect's attention, you do an "exposure," meaning you show them (expose them to) the information.

Don't explain the information, or do the presentation yourself. Use a "third party" tool like a DVD, website, recorded voice mail message, or a live event, where another distributor does the presentation.

("Third party" means anything or anyone but you.)

There are several reasons why it's best to use tools and events to show prospects the information.

The first reason is that the tools and events give distributors instant CREDIBILITY. A company produced video, for example, with professional production standards and the best speakers, is usually more impressive and persuasive than a distributor providing his or her summary of what the business is all about. Especially when the distributor is new and doesn't have a successful track record to point to.

The tools "remember" all the facts and deliver a professional presentation every time.

When you use third party tools, it doesn't matter what the prospect thinks about you, it's not about you. It's about the company, the products, and the opportunity.

The second reason we use tools and events to present the information is that it saves us a lot of TIME. Instead of spending 30-45 minutes with each prospect, you can give ten people a DVD or take 30 seconds to invite ten or twenty people to visit your website.

The third reason we use third party tools and events is DUPLICATION.

Duplication is the key to growing a big network marketing business. Duplication occurs when you use a *system* that anyone can use. A brand new distributor should be able to do the same thing their sponsor did with them.

Everyone can hand out a DVD. Not everyone can do a presentation.

Even if you can do the presentation, prospects will judge your business based on what they see you do. If you do something they think they can't do, or don't have the time to do, there's a good chance they won't sign up as a distributor.

If you do a 45 minute presentation with them, they will think they need to do a 45 minute presentation. What if they think they can't do that presentation? What if they think they wouldn't have the time?

If you go through a flip chart or a brochure with prospects and explain the business, they might think you did a great job, but if they don't think they can do what you did, they may say, "it's not for me".

If you hand them a DVD, however, or give them a web page to go to, or a phone number to dial and listen to a recorded message or live conference call, your prospects will see that this is something they can do.

In a traditional business, you do what works. In network marketing, you do what *duplicates*.

3. FOLLOW-UP AND CLOSE

Most people don't sign up as a distributor the first time they see some information. They may buy your product or service, but starting a business is a bigger decision. You will probably have to do more than one exposure before most prospects are ready to sign up in the business.

After each exposure, follow-up as soon as possible. If they tell you they will review your 30-minute DVD tonight at 8pm, follow-up with them at 8:35pm. If they are dialing into a conference call that will end at 6:30pm, you should follow-up with them at 6:31pm.

Too much time allows them to cool off, forget what they saw, or get distracted. The sooner you follow-up, the better. If possible, try to follow-up within 48 hours or less.

The first thing you do when you follow-up is find out if the prospect saw the information. Did they watch the video or listen to the call? If they didn't see it, find out when they can look at it and follow-up again.

If they did see it, find out if they are ready to sign up. If they are ready, sign them up. If they aren't ready, but they are interested, get them more information (do another exposure)—show them another website, invite them to your next conference call, or invite them to a live event. (You'll learn how to determine interest in a later chapter.)

You continue this process of doing exposures and follow-ups until the prospect signs up in the business and/or buys your product or service.

If they have questions, the best thing to do is to get them on the phone with your upline or another distributor via a 3-way call. Let them answer your prospect's questions, and, if they are ready, your upline will "close" them.

If a prospect isn't interested, generally speaking, you move on, at least for now.

ACTION STEPS/POINTS TO REMEMBER

- Call your prospects and tell the you want to show them something. If you're going to expose them over the phone, give them the information. (You'll learn how to do the exposure in a later chapter). If you're going to meet with them in person, schedule the day and time.

- Recruiting usually requires a series of exposures and follow-ups. When you follow up after a first exposure, make sure you do it as soon as possible.

- Continue exposing and following up with your prospects. If they're still interested, get them more information and/or invite them to a live event. When you think they might be getting ready to sign up, or they have questions, get them on the phone with your upline or another distributor.

3-PART DIRECT APPROACH

1. SHOW

2. 15 MINUTES

3. INTERESTED/NOT

There are two basic approaches: direct and indirect. In the direct approach, you tell the prospect that you want to show them something and suggest that it might interest or benefit them.

There are 3 parts to the direct approach.

1. SHOW

"I've got something to SHOW you. . ."

You want them to know that you have something to SHOW them, not something to tell them or explain to them. You say this because you want them to know it's something they need to see or hear, and to preclude them from asking questions before they've seen anything. By not telling them anything, you make them curious.

2. 15 MINUTES

"It will only take 15 MINUTES. . ."

Your first exposure with a prospect should usually be brief. Don't ask for an hour. Not everyone is willing to give you that much time, especially when they don't know what it is that you want to show them. Most people will give you 15 minutes, however, and that's usually enough for a first exposure.

If the video or presentation you intend to show them is longer than 15 minutes, just show them the *first* 15 minutes. If they like it and want to see more, that's fine. You have kept your "15 minute" promise.

If you plan to show them a 3 minute video or recorded message, tell them "it will only take 3 minutes."

3. INTERESTED/NOT

"You may or may not be INTERESTED. . ."

You want them to know that you're not going to give them a sales pitch or pressure them to do something. You do that by acknowledging up front that they may not be interested in what you show them and that a response of "not interested" is okay.

You're giving them person to say no.

You might word it differently, however. For example: "Don't worry, I'm not going to ask you to buy anything" or (with a smile in your voice) "You can leave your wallet at home".

You want them to know that you just want to show them something. Your friendship, or their curiosity, should be enough to get them to agree.

Of course, you want them to join your business or buy something, or at least ask for more information, but that will be their decision. Your job is to show them the information. If they are interested, great. If they aren't, that's fine, too.

Use words that feel natural to you. Leave out something if you want. Mix up the order.

Here are a few different ways you can do the approach:

"Hey Mary, do you have 15 minutes? There's something I want you to look at. . ."

"Hi Mary, do you have a few minutes? You may not be interested but I've got something I'd like to you listen to. . ."

"Mary, glad I caught you. If you have 15 minutes, I want to show you something I think you might like. . ."

"Hey Mary, I want to show you something cool I'm working on. It may not be your thing, but it will only take a few minutes to check it out. . .would it be okay if I dropped by later today?"

The key is that you want to *show* them something. If they ask, "What is it?" say, "That's what I want to show you!" or "It will be quicker to SHOW you," or, "I don't have time right now, I'll show you everything when I get there (i.e., to their house, if you've asked to come over), or, "Everything is explained on the video. . ."

ACTION STEPS/POINTS TO REMEMBER

- Learn the 3-part DIRECT approach. Practice it until you can deliver it smoothly.

- Practice different replies if they ask, "What is it?" or they say, "Just tell me what it's all about."

- Make sure you always have tools on hand that you can use for a brief exposure (i.e., under 15 minutes), and tools you can use if like what they see and want to see more, e.g., longer videos, websites, brochures, etc. Also, make sure you know the dates and times of any live presentations you can invite them to.

3-PART INDIRECT APPROACH

1. FAVOR/HELP

2. OPINION OR REFERRALS

3. THANK YOU

With a direct approach you tell the prospect you want to show them some information, suggesting that it might interest them or benefit them. With an indirect approach, you ask the prospect to look at the information as a *favor* to you.

1. FAVOR/HELP

The first part is simple. You tell them that you want or need their help, or ask if they would be willing to you a favor.

"Would you help me. . ?"

"I need to ask you a favor. . ?"

"If you've got a few minutes, I could use some help. . ."

2. OPINION/REFERRALS

The favor you're asking for is to look at something you're doing and give you their opinion. There's no pressure for them to do anything, you simply want to know what they think about what *you're* doing.

Most people like to give their opinion and are flattered that you asked them. They are also curious about what you're doing.

Of course you hope they like what you show them, and they want to buy something and/or become a distributor, but you don't suggest that during the approach. Let it be their idea, after they see the information.

Instead of asking for their opinion, you could ask for referrals. You might do this if the prospect owns a business or has a list of people who might be good prospects for your business or products.

It's a good idea to tell people why you are asking *them* for help. You might tell them that you value their opinion, because you know they are intelligent or because they are successful in their business or job. Or you might say that they are a good friend and you trust them to give you their honest opinion.

If you ask for referrals, point out that you know that they know a lot of people and they might be able to give you some referrals.

Here are some examples of an indirect approach:

"I've started a business and I want to show you what I'm doing and get your opinion. . ."

"I'm working on a business project and I'd love to get your feedback on something. . ."

"I've started a business and I want to show you what I'm doing. . . You might be able to refer a couple of people to me that I could talk to. . ."

"Would you help me? I'm working on something important and I'd like to get your opinion. . ."

3. THANK YOU

Always say please and thank you:

"Could you help me please? I would really appreciate it. Thank you so much . . ."

"Thank you; I knew I could count on you. . ."

"This really means a lot to me. . ."

Show them that you appreciate their help. This is more than just good manners, though. It reinforces the idea that they are helping you merely by looking at what you're doing.

Prospects tend to be more relaxed and open when they know you're not asking them to buy something, and since you know they will be more relaxed, you will be more relaxed, too.

If they aren't interested in what you show them, there are no hard feelings. You're thanking them for looking at the information and giving you their opinion, not for buying. You can always come back to them at another time.

Since you're asking for a favor, an indirect approach usually works best with your warm market (i.e., people you know).

An indirect approach is especially good when approaching prospects who are older or more successful than you (or see themselves that way). When you tell them that you admire them and their success, or that you look up to them and value their opinion, they are usually flattered that you are asking for their help.

ACTION STEPS/POINTS TO REMEMBER

- Try out different versions of the indirect approach with some prospects and see which ones you are most comfortable using.

- Tell your prospects why you are asking *them* for help. Tell them that you value their opinion, for example, or tell them that you know they know a lot of people through their business, their job, or through something else they do.

- Always say "please" and "thank you". Make sure they know that you appreciate their help.

3 TYPES OF EXPOSURES

1. PRODUCT/SERVICE

2. OPPORTUNITY

3. BOTH

Once you have approached a prospect and they have agreed to look at the information, what do you show them? Here are 3 options:

1. PRODUCT/SERVICE

Some distributors first show prospects information about their products or services, without any mention of the business opportunity. They want the prospect to buy and use the products and become a happy customer first, before they talk to them about the business opportunity.

The distributor may mention that there is a business opportunity, but not present the details until after the prospect has placed an order.

Some distributors will wait until the customer is about to place an order and then tell them that they can get those product(s) wholesale, i.e., by becoming a distributor.

The advantage of the "product first" approach is that it might bring in more sales for a new distributor from warm market contacts who are willing to make a purchase to help the distributor in their new business.

Also, some distributors are more comfortable talking about their products first. They find it easy to share with their friends how the products have helped them, for example.

One disadvantage of the "product first" approach is that the prospect might not want to order any products when you first approach them (for whatever reason), but if they knew about the business opportunity, and they were interested in that, they would probably be more likely to place a product order.

Another consideration is that if you offer a line of products, or different lines of products, you have to consider which product(s) or line(s) to show the prospect. They may not be interested in the product you show them, but be very interested in something else. Deciding what to show them, or making inquiries about what they might like to see, can confuse prospects and slow down the recruiting process.

2. OPPORTUNITY

Some distributors lead with the business opportunity. They talk to their prospects about earning more income, building retirement income, gaining time freedom, or starting their own business so they can be their own boss. They emphasize these benefits when they do exposures.

The advantage to this approach is that by leading with the opportunity, you will be more likely to sign up more business-minded distributors rather than customers who are primarily interested in the products, or at best, earning some "extra" income.

Your business will grow more quickly by signing up distributors who want to build a big business and make a lot of money.

If you lead with the business opportunity, you will, of course, also show prospects your products or services; they are central to the business. But you will lead with and *emphasize* the money and other benefits they can earn or achieve with your company.

3. BOTH

The simplest approach is to show prospects both the business opportunity and the products or services and let them decide what they are interested in. This also allows you to ask, after the exposure, "What did you like best, the [product], the business, or both?"

When you show both the business and the products to everyone, some people will order products, some will sign up in the business (and order products), and some will do neither but may give you referrals.

Whatever happens, at least they know that you offer *both* a business opportunity and a line of products or services. In the future, their interests or situation may change and they may then be interested in something you offer. Or they might meet someone who is looking for products like yours, or an opportunity to increase their income, and refer them to you.

ACTION STEPS/POINTS TO REMEMBER

- As you go through your list, in preparation for approaching prospects, decide what information or tool(s) you will show them first. Will you show them a product first? Which one? Will you lead with the opportunity? Or will you show them everything and let them decide. Talk to your upline about which approach they recommend.

- Eventually, you will probably find that you have a preferred method of approaching prospects. When you find what works best for you, stick with it.

- Make sure you always have a variety of tools on hand (or online), in case a prospect wants to know more about one of your products or about your business opportunity.

3 WAYS TO DO EXPOSURES

1. TOOLS

2. EVENTS

3. EXPERTS

Your first exposure with a prospect should be brief. 15 minutes or less. This allows you to quickly find out whether or not they are interested. It's also easier to get prospects to agree to look at or listen to the information when you're only asking for a few minutes of their time.

If they're not interested after a good ten minute exposure, the odds are they won't be interested after a one hour exposure. Save yourself some time and go talk to someone else.

If they are interested, however, you can do longer exposures. If they were interested after the first exposure, they'll watch a one hour presentation, not because you asked them to but because they're interested!

1. TOOLS

Tools include DVDs, online videos, live conference calls, recorded messages, printed materials, and so on. Here are some ways you can use these tools to do exposures, especially for a (brief) first exposure:

- Hand them a DVD and ask them to watch it that evening; if it is longer than 15 minutes, tell them to only watch the first 15 minutes

- Meet them at a coffee shop and play the DVD or a video on your website

- Ask them to dial into a recorded message. Tell them to "Grab a Pen" and write down the number you give them

- If you are in person with them, dial the number yourself and put it on speaker, or hand the phone to the prospect to listen

- Use the 3-way calling function on your phone to connect the prospect with the recorded voice mail message

- Mail a DVD or other tool with a note asking the prospect to watch the DVD and telling them you will be calling to get their feedback

- Call, make sure they have a few minutes to look at something, and then text them a link to your website video or the phone number for a recorded message

- Invite them to dial into a live conference call taking place that evening (or whenever)

2. EVENTS

Events are live presentations. They may be conducted remotely, via webinar or phone conference, but when we refer to events we usually mean those that are conducted in person. They usually take place at a hotel ballroom or conference room, an office, or a restaurant. They can also take place in a home.

The event may be called a "business overview," "business briefing," "company overview," "opportunity showcase," "executive luncheon," or something similar. These are generally open to any distributors in the local market (except those that take place at a distributor's home).

Events usually show the full presentation, that is, the company, the products or services, the business, and the compensation plan. At the end of the presentation, distributors share their stories or testimonials about the products, the business, or both.

The advantage of live events is that they allow prospects to see the presentation delivered by a top distributor, meet other distributors and hear their stories, get their questions answered, and experience all of excitement and energy in the room. They can also see actual products.

Another advantage of live events is that when prospects see other guests filling out paperwork and getting started in the business, it provides "social proof" of the value of the business. For this reason, prospects who might have previously been undecided often sign up at the events.

Live events can be used for a first exposure, but it's usually better to invite prospects who have already had one or more exposures. If they've been exposed, and they are interested, they will be more likely to show up when you invite them to an event, and more likely to sign up when they do.

3. EXPERTS

Another way to do an exposure is to invite a prospect to meet with your upline or other distributor. The other distributor is your "expert," but introduce them to the prospect as your business partner.

The expert may do the entire presentation or a shorter version.

They may sit with you and the prospect(s) while you watch a DVD or web video and then share additional information about the business. They may explain the comp plan, tell their success story, and answer questions. They will also find out if the prospect is ready to sign up.

You can use an expert to do the presentation at an in-person meeting (a "sit down") or over the phone. You can use them to do a first exposure, to invite a prospect to an event, or to answer your prospect's questions and close (help them decide to sign up).

ACTION STEPS/POINTS TO REMEMBER

- If you haven't already done so, choose one or two of each type of tool available to you as your primary first exposure tool. You might choose one DVD, one recorded phone message, and one website or online video.

- Attend your local recruiting events and introduce yourself to the leaders and as many other distributors as possible. Become familiar with the starting time, parking, sign-in process, and how the presentation is conducted. When you return with guests, you'll know what to do and you'll be able to introduce your guests to other distributors in the room.

- Find out which distributors in your upline are available for you to use as an expert. Learn their stories so you can more effectively introduce them to your prospects.

3 THINGS PROSPECTS WANT TO KNOW

1. BUSINESS

2. PRODUCTS

3. YOU

After you approach a prospect, they may ask you questions about your business or what you do. The best way to answer those questions is to do an exposure. Let the tools do the talking for you.

After an exposure, they may still have questions. The best way to handle their questions is to give them another tool (do another exposure), direct them to your website, or get them on the phone with another distributor to answer their questions.

You can answer basic questions if you know the answer, but it's better to let someone or something else answer most questions for you. That way, prospects will see that if they get involved in the business, they can get someone else to answer *their* prospect's questions.

Also, at some point you will be asked to answer questions for other distributor's prospects. You will be the other distributor's "expert".

By then, you should be able to answer the following types of questions:

1. BUSINESS

Prospects want to know what kind of business you are in. What do you do? What kinds of products or services do you offer? What is your target market and how big is it?

They also want to know how much money they can earn if they sign up in your business. How much could they earn part time, a few hours a week? How much could they earn full time?

You don't necessarily have to show them the entire comp plan but you should be prepared to give them a general idea of what's possible so they can decide whether they want to see more detailed information.

Prospects also want to know what they would have to do to earn that much. They want to know what distributors do each day. Do they have to go door to door? Is this sales? Are there quotas?

To a great extent, you answer this question when you do the approach and the exposure. You want prospects to see that what distributors do is something that *they* could do.

Show them that the business isn't difficult and doesn't take a lot of time.

After you have approached and exposed the prospect, if they ask you what they would have to do to earn money in your business, you want to be able to say, "Well, what did I do with you?" If you are answering questions for Mary, another distributor, and the prospect asks what they will have to do in the business, you can say, "Well, what did Mary do with you?"

You want the prospect to see that they could do this business.

If you (or Mary) handed the prospect a DVD and then got them on the phone with another distributor to answer their questions, the prospect will realize that they can do that, too.

2. PRODUCTS

Prospects want to know something about your products or services. They want to know that customers get valuable benefits from them.

What do your products do? What problems do they fix or prevent? How do they protect people, help them save money, or improve their life?

Do you have proof? Studies? Patents? Certifications? Be prepared to share the hard evidence and some success stories.

They also want to know what they get when they buy—how many in a bottle, how often do they use it, how do they access the service, and of course, the price. If your product is priced higher than other products in your market, you should be prepared to show them why your products are worth more.

Most of these questions should be answered in the presentation. You can also hand them a brochure, direct them to a web page, or get them on the phone with another distributor.

3. YOU/YOUR COMPANY

If you are in a competitive field, prospects want to know why they should buy from or sign up with your company.

How long has it been in business? Does it have experienced management? How is it better than or different from other companies in the field?

Do you offer unique products or solutions? Do you have any advantages in the market? Does the company offer distributors more than other companies (income, training, support, etc.)?

They may also want to know why they should sign up with *you* instead of another distributor. Will you spend more time with them or provide them with more support? If you're relatively new in the business, tell them your upline's story and how they have helped you and other distributors achieve success.

ACTION STEPS/POINTS TO REMEMBER

- Review your company's literature and websites so you will know where to find the information prospects usually want to know about your company, products, and business opportunity. Review the tools you plan to use, to see how they present this information.

- Talk to your upline and find out what your company and team offers distributors that may not be available with other companies or teams. What extra tools, training, leadership calls, or other help is available? Ask them to help you prepare to answer the question, "Why you?"

- Set up a "training notebook" and start writing down the most common questions prospects ask, and the answers you have found. This will prepare you to answer those questions for your prospects, and for your team's prospects.

3 WAYS TO DETERMINE INTEREST

1. THEY TELL YOU

2. ASK

3. ASSUME IT

After an exposure, you need to find out if the prospect is interested in what you have shown them.

If you do the exposure while you are physically with them, or on the phone with them, you can find out immediately. Otherwise, you need to follow up by contacting them again.

You want to find out if they are interested in what they've seen. If they are, you can show them more information, or find out if they are ready to buy your products or services, or sign up as a distributor. This can happen at any time—after one exposure or after ten exposures, and you should be prepared to sign them up or take their order at any time.

How will you know if they are interested? How will you know if they are ready to sign up?

1. THEY TELL YOU

Many prospects come right out and tell you they are interested in getting more information or they are ready to sign up. If they ask for more information, or if they tell you they want to get started, don't act surprised!

They may not come right out and say they want to sign up, but you can often tell. They might make a positive comment about your products or about your business. Or they may ask questions, which is usually a sign of interest.

If they ask about the products—sizes, ingredients, side affects, how to use them— for example, you know they are interested in the products. They may not be ready to buy, but they are interested, and that means you should move forward.

Get them more information or a product sample. Introduce them to someone who has used the product and had good results. Or simply ask if they are ready to place an order.

If they ask about getting paid, about setting up their website, or about ordering inventory, you know they are interested in the business. Offer them more information (e.g., give them another tool or invite them to a live event), introduce them to another distributor to answer their questions, or just ask them if they're ready to sign up.

2. ASK

If you're not sure if some is interested, ask them. After they have seen a tool or after the presentation at a live event, ask, "What did you like best?" or "What was your favorite part?"

Another question you can ask is, "Are you interested in the product, the business, or both?"

If they liked the money, introduce them to someone who is earning a lot of money with your company, or tell their story. If they liked the product and you have had success using the product yourself, tell them your story. If they liked "everything" ask them if they are ready to get started.

If they haven't seen a full presentation, or you're still not sure what they think, simply ask, "Would you like to get more information?"

If they say yes, it usually means they're interested (in something). Get them more information, invite them to another event, or introduce them to someone in your upline.

3. ASSUME IT

Sometimes, prospects won't tell you they are interested, even when you ask. They may want to think about it, or they may like what they've seen but not want you to know. People can be funny sometimes!

No problem. If they don't tell you they AREN'T interested, go ahead and assume that they are.

If they've seen a DVD, for example, invite them to your live event.

If they've listened to your conference call, send them the link to your website.

If you're with them at a presentation, introduce them to the speaker or a successful distributor in the room.

Continue to move forward, from exposure to exposure, until they tell you yes or they tell you no. (But see the upcoming chapter, "3 THINGS TO DO WHEN YOU GET A "NO".)

ACTION STEPS/POINTS TO REMEMBER

- Listen to what the prospect says or asks you during or after the presentation. Are they asking questions? Saying something positive? What are they asking about? What do they like?

- If you're not sure, ask them. "What did you like best?" or "What was your favorite part?"

- Unless they tell you they AREN'T interested, assume that they are (still) interested and do another exposure.

3 STEPS TO A SUCCESSFUL 3-WAY CALL

1. EDIFY

2. INTRODUCE

3. LISTEN

3-way calls allow new distributors to start signing up distributors immediately. All they (you) need to do is their show prospects some information (i.e., do one or more exposures) and then get them on the phone with another distributor via a 3-way call.

The other distributor will answer the prospect's questions, overcome objections, and invite them to get started.

The best way to learn how to close prospects (which you will eventually do for other distributors) is to listen to a more experienced distributor do it.

Here's how to do a 3-way call.

1. EDIFY

Before you introduce your prospect to another distributor, edify them, that is, say something nice about them to the prospect so that the prospect knows they are speaking with someone they should listen to and respect.

Privately, we refer to the other distributor as our "expert". When we speak to prospects, however, we refer to them as our "business partner". Or we might refer to them as, "Someone who is having a lot of success in the business".

You can edify your expert in terms of their accomplishments with the company. For example, you might say that they are "a top leader with your company" or they are "building one of the fastest growing organizations in the business".

You can also edify your expert in terms of their accomplishments outside of the company. If they are a professional, a business owner, an executive, or another successful career, their background is probably worth mentioning.

If the expert and the prospect have something in common—where they live or where they went to school, their occupation or industry, what they like to do for fun—it's can be helpful to also mention this to the prospect. When two people have something in common, they are more likely to relate to each other.

2. INTRODUCE

After you edify your expert to your prospect, the next step is to introduce them.

Don't just call your expert without first making sure they are available to speak with your prospect. Text them a few minutes before you call your prospect and ask if they are available. (It's best to have several distributors you can call, in case the first one isn't available).

If your expert is available, i.e., they respond to your text and tell you they can talk, put the prospect on hold and call the expert. Confirm that you have a prospect on hold and tell your expert something about them—how you know them, what they have seen or heard (tools, calls, events, websites), and what they like about what they've seen.

If the prospect has questions you want the expert to address, mention these, too.

When the expert gives you the go ahead, connect the three calls (you, the expert, and the prospect). You've already edified the expert, so all you have to do is introduce them.

The introduction is easy. Say something like, "Mr. Jones [your expert], I want to introduce you to my friend, Mary [your prospect]; Mary, this is Mr. Jones."

Don't introduce the expert by their first name. Introduce them as "Mr," "Miss," "Ms." or "Mrs," followed by their last name. This shows respect for the expert and reminds the prospect that they are speaking with someone important.

3. LISTEN

Once you have introduced the expert and the prospect, mute your phone, listen, and take notes. Someday you will be the expert for other distributors, and this is how you learn what to do.

Don't speak while the expert and prospect are speaking. Don't interrupt the expert, even if they forget something or they make a mistake. Wait until they bring you into the conversation, or turn the call over to you.

The expert will answer the prospect's questions, share a story or two, and see if the prospect is ready to get started. If they have any objections, the expert will handle them. If the prospect is ready to get started, the expert will close them and turn the call over to you to sign them up.

At the end of the call, thank the expert for their time and assistance.

If the expert tells you to sign up the prospect (as a result of the conversation), go ahead and do that immediately after the call. Don't ask the prospect if they have more questions or chat with them about how great the business is, sign them up.

If the prospect isn't ready to sign up and the expert tells you to get them additional information, send them the information and schedule a follow-up.

If the expert invites the prospect to come to a live event and then turns the call over to you, confirm with the prospect when and where you will pick them up, or when and where you will meet them at the event.

If the prospect is long distance from you, ask a distributor who attends that event (on your team or the speaker or meeting holder) to meet with your prospect at the event.

ACTION STEPS/POINTS TO REMEMBER

- Ask your upline to introduce you to distributors on the team why can do 3-way calls for you. Ask them the best times to reach them, and how they prefer for you to introduce them.

- Practice doing 3-way calls with your upline and/or other distributors before you do one with actual prospects. Take turns playing the part of the Distributor, Expert, and Prospect. Practice edification and the introduction.

- As soon as a prospect sounds like they are interested, put them on the phone with an expert. Listen, take notes, and let them help you sign them up.

For more on how to do a 3-way call, see my other book, *Recruit and Grow Rich*.

3 WAYS TO HANDLE A "NO"

1. THANK YOU

2. WHO DO YOU KNOW?

3. STAY IN TOUCH

What do you do when a prospect says no? You have 3 options.

1. THANK YOU

The simplest way to handle a "no" or "not interested" is to say thank you and move on. There's no point in trying to convince anyone that they *should* be interested. If they're not, they're not.

Your job is to show people the information and collect a decision. Some people will be interested, some won't. If they are interested but not ready to sign up, show them more information. If they aren't interested, talk to the next person on your list.

If you have to talk someone into signing up in the business, assuming you could do that, you would have to talk them into *doing* the business. Who needs that? You want to sign up people who are excited about the business, not people who sign up because you talked them into it.

There are lot of reasons why prospects say no. They may too busy. They may think they don't have the skills to be successful. They may not need money or want the benefits offered by your products or services. If they are legitimate reasons for saying no, you must accept them.

When someone tells you no, they are doing you a favor. They are letting you know that you shouldn't spend more time with them. Some people waste your time by making you think they are interested when they really aren't. It's much better to find out how they really feel.

If someone isn't interested, great! You no longer have to talk to them about it or follow-up with them; you can use this time to find people who *are* interested.

And yet, as you gain experience in the business, you will realize that some people say no not because they aren't interested, but because they misunderstood something, or because of fears or doubts about their ability to be successful in the business. Eventually, you'll learn how to recognize these "objections" and how to overcome them.

2. WHO DO YOU KNOW?

In addition to thanking the prospect for taking a look at the information, ask them for referrals. They may know someone who needs your product or service, or someone who wants to earn more income.

Ask *everyone* for referrals, and keep it simple:

"Who do you know who might want to take a look at this?"

You'll learn more about referrals in **PART 3**.

3. STAY IN TOUCH

Some people say no because the timing isn't right for them. But things change and you should contact them again in a few months, to see if their situation or the timing has changed.

A prospect who isn't interested in your business today may be very interested in a few months or a few years. Stay in touch with people who tell you no.

Today, a prospect may not need extra income. Tomorrow, they may lose their job. A few months from now, they might have their hours cut and need more income. Or incur additional expenses they didn't anticipate. They might develop a health issue and realize they would be better off working from home.

There are many reasons why someone's circumstances may change. When someone tells you no, always assume it means "not now".

Contact them again in 90 days and see how they're doing. Update them on how you are doing in the business and ask them if they want to take another look.

When you reach another level in the compensation plan, or achieve another milestone in the business, let them know. People share good news with friends and family, so let them know.

If your company comes out with a new product, share that news. Ask them if they would like to take another look, or ask them for referrals.

Stay in touch with your prospects every few months. Keep it light and friendly and never push. Even though they told you no, you never know when they might be willing to take another look at your business, buy your products, or give you referrals.

ACTION STEPS/POINTS TO REMEMBER

- When someone says no, don't try to convince them; accept it, say thank you, and move on. Go talk to more prospects and find the ones who are excited about joining your business.

- In time, you will learn to recognize when a prospect is offering an objection that can be overcome (by your expert) and may still be interested. You will also learn how to overcome those objections when you are someone's expert.

- Stay in touch with everyone who says no. A no today can become a yes tomorrow.

PART III

GETTING TO THE NEXT LEVEL

You've learned the basics of getting your business started and getting your first distributor.

PART 3 is about building your team.

You'll learn how to get new distributors started right.

You'll learn how to get better at recruiting.

You'll learn how to find more prospects.

You'll learn how to start developing your leadership skills and take your business to the next level.

3 THINGS TO DO WHEN YOU GET A "YES"

1. START

2. SUPPORT

3. RECRUIT SOMEONE THEY KNOW

Congratulations! Someone said yes and signed up as a distributor.

Here are 3 things you should do. (If you're new, get your sponsor or upline to help you.)

1. START

Help your new distributor get started. Take them through the same process you went through when you got started. Get them signed up for the company or team training.

Show them the tools. Give them some samples. Help them order inventory.

Show them how to fill out the paperwork. Show them how to navigate their website. Make sure they calendar the days and times for company and team conference calls and local events.

Answer their questions and show them where to get information. Show them where to find the comp plan on the company website, how to order tools and inventory, and how to access the calendar. Show them where to find the documents they will need, where to find their earnings and other statistics.

Schedule their "game plan". Go over their list with them, schedule their launch event(s), and develop a plan of action for helping them approach people on their list.

Make sure they are using the products or services. You want them to fall in love with the products and what they can do. Help them develop a product story, so they can tell prospects how the products have helped them.

Introduce them to as many other distributors as possible, so they can hear their stories, be inspired by what's possible, and feel like they are part of a team.

Get them to the next live event where they can hear leaders speak, meet more people and hear more stories, and see the big picture.

2. SUPPORT

As your new distributor is getting started, you (and your upline) should support them. Teach them, protect them, and help them learn the business.

Go with them to the training and other events, to show them your support and to show them that they should do this with their distributors. Let them know that you are a team and you work together.

Offer to speak to their prospects, in person and via 3-way call. Tell their prospects your story and stories of other distributors you've met. Tell them how you have used the products. Tell them what excites you about the business. Tell them about the team and how they have helped you. Say something nice about the distributor who introduced you.

Eventually, you'll help them close their prospects.

As your distributors sign up their own distributors and advance in the business, you will support your growing team by staying in touch with them, keeping them informed about promotions and contests, and promoting upcoming events.

Encourage your distributors. Tell them stories about other distributors who are having success. Hold their hand when they have a bad day. Congratulate them when they make a sale, sign up a distributor, or move up to a new level.

Support your team by letting them know you want them to succeed and helping them do that.

3. HELP THEM GET THEIR FIRST RECRUIT

Your number one objective with a new distributor is to help them recruit *their* first distributor. If you do this with every distributor you recruit, your organization will continually grow.

Every new distributor on your team, whether you recruited them yourself or someone on your team recruited them, is a gateway to people you don't know. Ask your distributors to introduce you to the top people on their list. Work with your distributors and help them recruit people on their list.

If you recruit Bill, help Bill recruit Mary. Work with Mary and help her recruit her first distributor, Linda. Then, work with Linda and help her recruit her first distributor.

Continue working with the new distributors on your team, no matter who recruited them, no matter how deep in your organization they might be.

You want your organization to grow deep, with many levels of leaders. This makes your organization stronger because you will have many levels of distributors. As they recruit and build their team, your organization will grow deeper and more secure.

You also want to continue to recruit new front line distributors. This gives you additional profitability.

Continue building deep (working with your down-line team) and building wide (recruiting new distributors/starting new "legs").

ACTION STEPS/POINTS TO REMEMBER

- Get your new distributor to the next training and schedule their game plan. If you're brand new, ask your sponsor or someone in your upline to help you.

- Help your new distributor recruit their first distributor. Then help that distributor recruit their first distributor.

- Build your team deep, for security, and wide for profitability. Continue working with your team and recruiting new front line distributors.

3 WAYS TO USE EVENTS

1. TEAM

2. PROSPECTS

3. YOU

Network marketing is an event-driven business. We use events to recruit and sell products, and to train distributors and inspire them to get to the next level.

Here are 3 ways to use events to build your business.

1. TEAM

Events include business presentations and trainings. Both help distributors re-sell themselves on the business. They hear news about the company and the products, meet other distributors and hear their success stories, and watch top distributors do the presentations and conduct the trainings.

Events also allow you and your team to watch and listen to successful distributors speaking to their prospects and their team. That's how distributors learn how to speak to their prospects and their teams.

At the events, you can introduce your prospects (guests) to other distributors. They will share their story with your guests, answer their questions, and help them decide to get started.

After the events, distributors often go for coffee or a meal with other distributors in the local market, and with prospects. Distributors get to know each other better, share their goals and tips and stories, make friends, find workout partners, and support each other.

The best way to grow your team is to encourage them to attend the weekly and monthly events, and the events after the events. Each event reminds them that they made a good decision to get started and gives them impetus for the week or month ahead.

Attend the events in your local market and teach your team to do the same.

2. PROSPECTS

More prospects sign up as distributors at group events (e.g., business presentations in a hotel conference room) than sign up in a one-on-one setting.

It's not hard to understand why.

Prospects see a complete business presentation from a top distributor, with no other distractions. They hear testimonials from real people who share their experiences with the products and the business. And they see other guests signing up, which compels them to do the same.

After your prospects have had one or more exposures, if they still haven't signed up, invite them to a live presentation.

Introduce them to other distributors, so they can hear their stories and feel more comfortable. Get them a seat up front and sit next to them. Let them see you paying attention to the speaker, laughing at his or her jokes, and otherwise showing them that you respect the speaker and the information being presented, suggesting that they should, too.

Have paperwork and pens ready to hand to your guests at the end of the presentation. If they have questions, introduce them to the speaker or another leader in the room.

Invite your prospects to the after event. They'll be more relaxed, spend time with you and your team and other distributors in this less formal setting. Many prospects who aren't ready to sign up at the event itself often make the decision to sign up at the event after the event.

The best way to get guests to come to any event is to pick them up. The more guests you and your team have at each event, the bigger your business will grow.

3. YOU

We attend the events each week to get the same benefits we want for our team. At the events we learn the business and re-sell ourselves on the products and opportunity.

Each presentation, each training, provides us with information and stories we can use not only with our local team and prospects but with our long distance team and prospects. This week, at your local event, you might meet a school teacher. Next week, you might be speaking to a prospect who is also a teacher and you can tell her about the teacher who signed up last week. Even better, you might introduce the two teachers over the phone.

The events also keep us motivated. There is an energy in the room we don't experience when we are making calls from our home office. We are surrounded by other people who are on the same journey and we are inspired by their success.

When you have a bad week, you will find that you need the events. You need to be around other distributors who understand what you're going through. When you have a good week, the events need you. Other distributors need to hear your stories and be encouraged by them.

The weekly events also help you build momentum for the upcoming week. During the week leading up to the event, you invite guests to the next business presentation. You also promote that event to your team, encouraging them to invite guests to come hear the speaker and to meet you and other distributors.

ACTION STEPS/POINTS TO REMEMBER

- Find out where the local events take place in your market and put these on your calendar. If you have team in other markets, note these, too. Attend all of your weekly and monthly events and remind your team that you'll "see them there".

- Invite guests (prospects) to your local business presentations. Circle up with them after the presentation and sign them up.

- Meet with your team after business presentations and training events. Encourage them, recognize their achievements, and promote the next event.

3 KEY LEADERSHIP SKILLS

1. PROMOTING

2. RECOGNITION

3. 3-WAY CALLS (EXPERT)

> *"If your actions inspire others to dream more, learn more, do more and become more, you are a leader."* – John Quincy Adams

1. PROMOTING

One of the most valuable skills in network marketing is the skill of promoting. Promoting is leadership in action. Promoting means getting people to do things they might otherwise not do, or do as much or as consistently.

In network marketing, we promote:

- **Events.** The more prospects your team has at business presentations, the more your business grows. The more distributors you have at trainings and big events, the more your team produces and recruits.

- **Tools**. Promoting tools gets more prospects watching videos, listening to conference calls, and visiting websites. The more who watch, the more who sign up.

- **People.** You promote the speakers and trainers and your upline, by edifying them—saying nice things about them that make people more likely to trust them, listen to them, and follow them.

- **Contests.** If your company or your team is running a promotion or contest, you'll get more distributors to recruit more and sell more products by promoting the promotion.

- **Behavior.** When you promote the habit of daily activity, your team will develop better habits. When you promote the team calls, more of your team will get on the calls. When you promote consistency, your team will be more consistent.

Promoting doesn't mean "announcing". Promoting means helping people feel excited about achieving something important to them.

Promoting is a skill and it can be learned. Whatever it is that you are promoting, start by showing people that *you* are excited about it and you are "going for it" yourself.

Talk about the benefits—money, recognition, prizes, bragging rights, etc.

Create a sense of urgency by pointing out time limits, expiration dates, and price increases. As you get closer to the deadline, remind them that time is running out.

Share stories about what other distributors are doing, or have done, and how they are moving up the ranks and earning more income.

Ask for your team's commitment to doing the activity or qualifying for the promotion.

Encourage them and share your expectations. "I know you can do it," "I'm counting on you to set the example," "I'm excited about seeing you their."

Help them by offering to coach them, make calls with them, and talk to their prospects or team.

2. RECOGNITION

When a distributor on your team earns their first sale, signs up their first distributor, advances in rank, or qualifies for a promotion or award, congratulate them and share their achievement with others on the team.

Recognizing what they have done tells them you are proud of them. It makes them feel good about themselves and inspires them to work towards additional achievements.

In addition to recognizing their results, recognize their efforts. Compliment them on the number of exposures they have done, the number of guests they invited to the weekly event, or the number of prospects they put on the phone to speak with you or your upline.

Continually look for reasons to notice your distributors doing something right. If they showed up early at the event, let them know that you noticed. When they have a guest at the event, talk to the guest and say something nice to them about the distributor who invited them. If your distributor does a testimonial at the event, tell them they did a great job.

When you recognize distributors in front of other distributors, those other distributors will surely congratulate them too. They will also be motivated to do more themselves, to earn your recognition and praise.

Post your distributor's achievements on your team Facebook page, mention it in your email newsletter, or make a fuss about it on your team call.

Share your team's accomplishments with your upline leaders, so they can join in the congratulations.

Recognition is a powerful tool for bonding with your team and inspiring them to reach higher levels of success.

3. 3-WAY CALLS (EXPERT)

You've been introducing your prospects to other distributors (your expert) over the phone. You know how to edify an expert and introduce them. You've listened to the expert speak with your prospects.

You heard how the expert builds rapport by asking prospects about their background, where they went to school, and what they like about your business and products.

You've heard the expert answer the prospect's questions, finds out if they're ready to sign up, and closes. You've hear them invite prospects to an event to get more information.

You've listened and taken notes. You realize that prospects usually ask the same questions and experts usually tell the same stories. You've also seen that when a prospect is ready, closing them often requires little more than asking, "Are you ready to get started?"

You have put twenty or thirty prospects on the phone with an expert and you realize that you can do what they do.

Soon, you will.

At first, you'll simply share your story with your distributor's prospects. You'll tell them why you got started and what you like about the business.

Eventually, you'll ask, "Are you ready to get started?" and you'll be closing your team's prospects.

ACTION STEPS/POINTS TO REMEMBER

- Listen to how your upline leaders promote. Take notes. Use what you learn with your team.

- Listen to how your upline leaders praise and recognize their team. Ask for their suggestions for awards and contests you might use with your team.

- Get together with a workout partner or your upline and practice doing 3-way calls as the expert. Keep doing 3-way calls with your prospects and learn more about how to do these calls as an expert for your team.

For more on how to do a 3-way call, see *Recruit and Grow Rich*.

3 TYPES OF DISTRIBUTORS

1. LEADERS

2. LINKS

3. CUSTOMERS

You will sign up 3 types of distributors in your business, and so will your team. Here's what you need to know about them.

1. LEADERS

Every successful network marketing business is built through the leadership of a relative small number of distributors.

You don't need to find or develop hundreds of leaders. You only need a few.

Those leaders will find other leaders. And help those leaders find more.

In this way, you and a few other distributors can build an organization of thousands.

It works the same way in the corporate world. A big company with thousands of employees has one CEO and a senior management team usually numbering fewer than 30 executives. These top-level leaders work with lower-level leaders (e.g., managers, department heads, supervisors, etc.), who lead and manage their departments or divisions.

What is a leader? John C. Maxwell says that leadership is, "Influence; nothing more, nothing less." A leader, then, is someone who influences other people—to dream bigger, do more, and achieve more.

When you see someone in your organization who is working the business without depending on you, you know you have a leader.

You helped them get started, you supported them and encouraged them, and they took the initiative to build their business.

And you only need a few of these self-motivated people to build a huge organization.

You will have to sign-up and work with many distributors to find your leaders. You may find that you recruited them, or you may find them many levels deep in your organization. Wherever you find them, stay close to them, help them, encourage them, but don't get in their way.

As they build their business, they will also build yours.

2. LINKS

Most distributors aren't leaders. But every distributor in your organization can lead you to leaders.

A distributor may sign up only one distributor who turns out to be a leader. Or they may sign up a distributor and *they* might be a leader.

Everyone can be a link to a leader. Even prospects can be a link to leaders through their referrals. Prospect Joe refers you to Mary, Mary refers you to John, John refers you to Ellen who signs up and then recruits Sally, who goes out and build a big team. Joe, Mary, John, and Ellen are links. Sally is the leader.

You never know who will become a leader or lead you to one. Work with your new distributors and find out who they know. When they sign up someone, work with them and find out who *they* know.

You may find a leader ten levels deep in your organization. Or twenty or thirty. Be on the lookout for them. They can lead you to other leaders and build a big organization.

3. CUSTOMERS

Many distributors sign up with the best of intentions, but do nothing. They don't recruit or sell anything and they don't lead you to anyone.

Or they sign up as a distributor simply to obtain the products or services wholesale or at a "dealer discount".

That's okay. As long as they buy something from you or someone on your team, they are contributing to your income.

Your non-working distributors may also provide you with referrals. These referrals may buy something or become a distributor.

Customers, no matter where they come from, can lead you to more customers, and to distributors.

And someone who is "only" a customer today may become a distributor six months or six years from now. Stay in touch with your customers and inactive distributors. You can sign up a lot of distributors that way.

ACTION STEPS/POINTS TO REMEMBER

- Get to know the leaders in your upline. Spend time with them. Study them. Learn from them. Keep an eye out for people like them among your prospects and on your team.

- The first step to becoming a leader is to become a model

distributor. Do all the activities, come to all the events, commit to getting the results. Become the person you want to attract.

- Start reading books about leadership. Ask your upline for recommendations.

3 KEYS TO MORE EFFECTIVE RECRUITING

1. QUANTITY

2. QUALITY

3. POSTURE

Recruiting is the key to building a big network marketing business. The more you and your team recruit, the bigger your organization and income will grow.

There are 3 factors that affect your recruiting.

1. QUANTITY

You may not be a top leader in your company, but if you are a good recruiter, you can reach the top of the compensation plan and achieve all of your income goals.

As you know, not everyone your recruit will be a leader. Most distributors also won't become top recruiters or producers. But when you recruit lots of distributors, you will find big recruiters and leaders and producers.

You will also have many distributors who don't do much in the business, but they do something. If you have 1000 distributors on your team who do only one sale per month, that's a lot of production in your organization you are overriding.

Building a bigger team through recruiting also gives you security. When you have a big team with lots of distributors, it won't matter if someone isn't recruiting or producing sales. It won't matter if someone quits. You'll have many others in your organization who are working the business.

How do you recruit more distributors? You talk to more prospects.

You approach and expose as many people as possible, as quickly as possible. Show them some information and find out if they are interested. If they are, show them more information (invite them to the next exposure). If they aren't, go talk to someone else.

Recruiting lots of distributors is as simple as talking to lots of prospects. You don't have to be that good to be a good recruiter. Talk to more people.

When everyone else is approaching one or two people, go talk to ten. Some will be interested, some won't, but the more you talk to, the more you will recruit.

Recruit as many people as you can and teach your team to do the same.

To learn how to recruit quickly and in large numbers see, *Recruit and Grow Rich.*

2. QUALITY

Anyone can be successful in network marketing. Anyone can build a big business. But some types of people tend to have more potential than others.

If someone has built a successful network marketing business in the past, the odds are that they can do it again. Small business owners, professionals, and people with a sales background are more likely to have the skills and contacts needed to build a successful network marketing business.

As you get started in the business, approach everyone you know. Quantity will lead to quality. But at some point, consider focusing on recruiting people who have already demonstrated the skills and work habits associated with building a business.

Recruit professionals and business owners and sales people. Recruit the sharpest, most successful people you can find.

Don't ignore your 18 year old neighbor who works at a fast food restaurant. What he lacks in skills he might make up for with determination and hard work. He might also lead you to professionals and business owners in his family.

Don't ignore the stay-at-home moms you know, or anyone else you know. Anyone can be successful in this business. But when you venture into the cold market, focus on finding and recruiting professionals, business owners, network marketers, and other people who already know how to build a business.

To learn more about recruiting professionals and other high-probability prospects, see my other book, *Recruiting Up*.

3. POSTURE

"Stand up straight," your mom told you. She knew that good posture was not only good for the health of your spine, it made you look more confident and attractive.

In the world of business, posture is more than just how you sit or stand. It is an attitude that tells people you believe in yourself and what you are doing. It tells them that you know where you are going and you know that you will get there.

When you have good posture, recruiting and team building is easier. You look confident, destined to be successful, and most people find these to be attractive qualities.

You've met people with good posture before. They have a firm handshake and a genuine smile. They make eye contact when they speak to you. When you speak to them, you somehow know that they are on their way to accomplishing great things.

In network marketing, when you have this posture, your prospects want to talk to you and find out what you're doing. They tend to be more positive about what you show them, and are more likely to join you on your journey.

Look at the top recruiters and top money earners in your company and you will see people with good business posture.

The good news is that anyone can develop this posture. Age or background don't matter. Experience doesn't matter. What matters is that you believe in what you are doing and you are confident that you will achieve your goals.

If you're not there yet, pretend that you are. "Act as if" you had those beliefs and that confidence. Yes, fake it until you make it!

Never apologize for asking for a prospect's time. You've got something exciting to show them, something that can completely change their life!

Let prospects know that while you'd love to work with them in the business, you don't need them to do it. Again, you know you where you are going and you know you will get there, with or without them.

Successful people are busy, and you should be, too. Always be busy. Always be in a hurry. Let people know you don't have a lot of time, you've got many other people to talk to. You have lots of people who are excited about what you're doing and want to see more.

As you achieve success in your business, your posture will grow naturally. Along the way, you can develop your posture by surrounding yourself with people who have it, both in your business (the top recruiters, money earners and other leaders in your company), and outside your business.

Networking with professionals and business owners, for example, will help you build your skills and confidence. Listen to what they say and how they say it. Observe their body language. Pay attention to the little things they do, and model their behavior. (You'll also meet some great prospects this way.)

Read biographies of successful business people. Attend personal development seminars. Attend all of the trainings that are available and continually improve your knowledge and skills.

The best recruiters and biggest income earners in network marketing make personal development a priority for themselves and their teams.

ACTION STEPS/POINTS TO REMEMBER

- Focus on recruiting as many distributors as possible and teach your team to do the same. Talk to lots of prospects, but don't spend a lot of time with people who aren't interested.

- Focus on recruiting quality prospects—professionals, sales people, business owners, and executives.

- Develop your business posture by associating with successful people in and out of your company, and through continual training and personal development.

3 KEYS TO FASTER RECRUITING

1. SORTING

2. PHONE

3. FOLLOW-UP

Recruiting faster helps you to get promoted faster and find leaders faster. As your team also recruits faster, the growth of your organization starts to compound, and so does your income.

Here are 3 keys to faster recruiting.

1. SORTING

Sorting means working quickly through a list of prospects to find the ones who are interested in your business. It means spending less time with those who aren't interested, so you have more time to spend with the ones who are.

Imagine you have a list of 100 prospects. Let's say that 70 of those people have no interest at all in your business (although they might buy your product or service). Of the remaining 30, let's say that 20 are somewhat interested, 10 are very interested, and of those 10, 5 are excited and ready to sign up right now.

You want to find those 5 and sign them up as soon as possible. The sooner you do, the sooner they can start building their business.

Sorting means moving quickly through your list and collecting decisions. Either they are interested or they aren't. Sorting means "not convincing". You don't try to talk them into being interested, you simply want to know if they are or they are not.

If they tell you they aren't interested, great! They just did you a favor by letting you know you shouldn't waste more time with them. If you accept this graciously and move on, you can always go back to them at a later time, when their circumstances may have changed.

The key to sorting is to "detach from the outcome". That means not caring whether any individual prospect is or isn't interested. You don't need anyone to be interested. You know that if you sort through enough people, you will find the ones who are.

Move quickly through your list and find them. Don't worry about anyone else.

2. PHONE

The best way to sort through a list of prospects is to use the phone. Email or text is okay to tell people you want to talk to them, but don't tell them why until you talk on the phone or meet in person.

You need to talk to people. You need to make sure you have their attention. You want them to hear the excitement and urgency in your voice.

Use the phone to find out if they are available to look at some information right now. If they can't, find out when they can look and schedule another conversation or meeting.

It would be great to meet with everyone in person, but there isn't time. Not if you are sorting. Not if you want to recruit quickly.

The best way to sort is to use the phone to find out if they are interested before you meet with them.

Let them listen to a brief recorded message, or direct them to a short video. If they don't like what they see or hear, you won't have to meet with them and you've just saved yourself a lot of time. If they do like it, invite them to see more videos or get on a conference call, or invite them to meet you in person.

3. FOLLOW-UP

A key to faster recruiting is to follow-up as soon as possible after each exposure. A key to more effective follow-up is schedule the follow-up at the time you do the exposure.

Before you hang up the phone, or say goodbye if you are in person, find out (a) when they will watch the video, visit the web site, or listen to the call, and (b) set up a day and time when you will call them to follow-up.

This will make it much more likely that they will do what they said they would do.

If you don't schedule the follow-up at the time of the exposure, when you contact them again you will often find that they didn't go to the website, watch the video, or listen to the conference call. So, you have to follow-up again.

Or you leave a message but they don't call you back. So you call again, perhaps several times, to find out if they saw the information.

You keep calling and leaving messages, or you reach them and they tell you they still haven't done it.

It's frustrating and a waste of time.

Most of this can be avoided by scheduling the follow-up in advance. Find out when they will watch your video, for example, and when you can call them to find out what they thought. Tell them you are putting this on your calendar and ask them to do the same.

Repeat it back to them: "So you'll be able to go to the website tonight after dinner, around 8, right? And I'll be calling you tomorrow night at 7:30 sharp, okay?"

Get them to acknowledge these two "appointments". They will be much more likely to do what they said they will do when they know you will be calling.

ACTION STEPS/POINTS TO REMEMBER

- You'll recruit faster by sorting through your list and collecting decisions. Your prospects are either interested or they are not. Show them a short video or recorded message and find out if they like what it and want to see more. If not, move on.

- The phone is the best way to sort. You can expose your prospects quickly and only meet them if they like what they see or hear and want to see more.

- Always ask prospects to tell you when they will look at the information. After every exposure, schedule the follow-up (date and time). Put this on your calendar and ask your prospects to do the same.

3 WAYS TO FIND MORE PROSPECTS

1. REFERRALS

2. NETWORKING

3. SOCIAL MEDIA

To recruit more distributors you need to keep your pipeline of prospects full. There are many ways to find prospects. Here are 3 free, easy ways to find more prospects that anyone can use.

1. REFERRALS

One of the best ways to continually find prospects is through referrals. Everyone knows people you don't know and if you ask, many people will give you referrals.

Not everyone will give you referrals, of course, but some people will readily give you five or ten or more. If you ask everyone for referrals, and you average only *one* referral per person, you will never run out of prospects.

Asking for referrals for your business can be as simple as saying,

"Who do you know who might want to earn more income?" or "If you were in my shoes, who would you talk to about this?"

For referrals for your product or service, you can ask, "Who do you know who might want to take a look at this?" or "Who do you know who might want a free sample?"

You can also ask for referrals to people with a specific occupation or background. For example, you could ask, "Who do you know who owns a small business?" or "Who do you know who is an insurance agent?"

Get in the habit of asking everyone for referrals. The more you ask for referrals, the more referrals you'll get.

2. NETWORKING

There are two types of networking: formal and informal.

You do informal networking when you go about your normal day. You meet people while you are running errands, at your children's dance or sporting events, at the bank, at church, at work, and everywhere else.

If you meet them at their place of business, ask for their card. If you meet them elsewhere, start a conversation and then give them a tool (DVD, magazine, etc.) and ask for their phone number or email.

Or, ask what they do for a living and then ask if they have a business card.

Another thing you can do is to say, "Do you mind if I give you my card?" Most people will say yes, if for no other reason than to be polite. As you hand your card to them, say something like, "I own a business and I'm looking for some people who might want to earn some extra income. If you know anyone, would you give them my card?"

If they say, "sure," you know they probably aren't a prospect. If they ask you, "What do you do?" or "What kind of business?" or something like that, you can say, "Do you know someone or are you interested for yourself?"

If they say they might be interested themselves, either give them a tool (and get their contact information), or tell them you don't have time to talk right now but you would be happy to send them some information and then get their email or phone number.

Formal networking means joining groups and attending their meetings. You meet other people each week and if it's a business-oriented group, you have the opportunity to tell each other about your business, or your products or services, and what types of customers or prospects you're looking for.

With community, social, school, or hobby groups, you meet people with whom you share an interest. Because of that shared interest, those people are more likely to relate to your story about why you started your business and willing to look at your information.

3. SOCIAL MEDIA

Another easy way to find prospects is on social media. You can look at their profile and learn something about their business and personal life before you connect with them and approach them about your business.

You can also participate in groups, where like-minded people share a common interest.

Don't look at social media as a way to advertise your business but as a way to expand your warm market by networking online.

Post about good things that are going on in your life, but avoid direct pitches about your business or products.

When one of your online connections or followers posts something that suggests they might be open to earning more income, you can contact them privately and offer them some information. If someone mentions a problem that your products or services address, you can tell them how your product has helped you or someone you know.

Over time, as you get to know your friends and followers and earn their trust, you can approach them as you would if you were networking in person.

Social media allows you to meet an almost endless number of prospects, in your home town or anywhere in the world.

ACTION STEPS/POINTS TO REMEMBER

- Ask everyone for referrals. Everyone knows people you don't know and most are willing to give you referrals.

- Prospects are everywhere. Make sure you always carry business cards and tools with you whenever you are out.

- Use social media primarily for networking and expanding your warm market, not to advertise your business or products.

3 KEYS TO BUILDING A BIG ORGANIZATION

1. DO IT FIRST

2. FIND A FEW

3. DON'T STOP

The ultimate goal of many distributors is to have a big organization with thousands of distributors and multiple leaders and a steady stream of passive income whether they continue to work or not.

When you have that, you have time freedom.

It's not easy to get there, and it doesn't happen overnight, but anyone can do it. Here are 3 keys to building a big organization.

1. DO IT FIRST

The key to building a big organization is to build your business in a duplicable way, and duplication starts with you.

Your team will do what you do, not what you say. If you want them to follow a duplicable system, they have to see you follow that system.

It has been said that when you sign up a new distributor, 80% of their training is done. They saw how you approached them. They heard what you said. They watched what you did to recruit them and that's how they believe the business is done.

If you did it right, they will be more likely to do it right. If you used tools and events to show them the information, if you got them on the phone with an "expert" to answer their questions, if you got yourself out of the way and showed them a simple system anyone can follow, they will be more likely to follow that system and duplicate what you did.

They'll be more likely to do it that way with their prospects. When those prospects get started, they'll do it with their prospects, because that's what they saw their sponsor do, and the system will continue to duplicate throughout your organization.

If you didn't do it right, if you "told" them all about the business, that's what they will do. If you did things they can't do, they may try, and give up, or never try at all.

If you don't go to the events, they won't go. If you go only occasionally, you can't expect them to do more. If you don't use 3-way calls to close them, they won't either.

Your team is watching what you do. Show them the system you want them to follow. Model the behavior you want to duplicate.

If you want your team to follow a system that duplicates, you must do it first.

2. FIND A FEW

Even when you follow the system consistently, even though you show your team the right way to build the business, not everyone will follow suit.

Some will do it, but not be consistent. They won't follow the system every time. Some will think they know a better way and not follow the system at all. Some will get bored doing things the same way and change things.

The distributors who build a big organization, however, are the leaders who consistently follow the system.

The good news is that you don't need everyone on the team following the system to build a big organization. You only need a few.

You will find a few leaders on your team who commit to following the system. You work with them and help them find a few leaders who do the same.

It's called "working with the willing".

As your team gets bigger, you can't give everyone the same amount of your time. Invest most of your time working with the ones who commit to following the system.

How do you know who that is? Watch what they do.

Not what they say but what they do.

They are the ones who, when they get started, call you and ask lots of questions. You don't have to chase them or talk them into coming to the events or getting on the calls, they do it on their own.

They are the ones who consistently approach prospects, show them the information, and put them on the phone with you.

Many distributors say they are excited and tell you what they plan to do. That's fine. But give most of your attention to the ones who actually do it.

In the beginning, they may not get great results. That's okay. If they continue doing the activities and following the system, the results will come.

3. DON'T STOP

Every network marketing organization has attrition. Distributors quit, even ones who are making lots of money.

They may believe they have done enough and not want to do any more. They might think the grass is greener in another company and leave yours. They may become ill or die or wish to retire. Or they may find something else they want to do.

You have to be prepared for attrition in your business.

Don't stop recruiting new front line distributors into your organization. Don't stop working with your downline leaders. Don't stop building your business until you are truly ready to retire or move onto something else.

You can slow down if you want to. If you've been working hard for several years and you want to enjoy some of the fruits of your labor, go ahead. You deserve it.

But don't quit until you are "done".

ACTION STEPS/POINTS TO REMEMBER

- Set an example for your team by following the system, consistently. Show them what to do by doing it first.

- Find a few leaders on your team who commit to following that system and work with them. Help them find a few leaders who are willing to do the same.

- Don't stop until you're done. Don't get into "management mode"—continue to recruit and build your business until you're ready to retire or move onto something else.

3 REASONS DISTRIBUTORS STRUGGLE

1. NOT DOING IT RIGHT

2. NOT DOING IT ENOUGH

3. LACK OF BELIEF

There are 3 reasons distributors struggle in network marketing:

1. NOT DOING IT RIGHT

When a distributor isn't getting the results they want it is often because they aren't doing the right activities, or they aren't doing them the right way.

When they approach prospects they might "explain" the business, instead of letting the tools do the talking for them. They might be good at approaching prospects and doing exposures but drop the ball when it comes to follow-up. They might try to convince people who aren't interested that they should be interested, annoying them and wasting time.

If you find yourself struggling with some aspect of the business, record yourself and listen to how you sound. Are you saying the right things? Are you talking too much? Are you listening to what the prospect says and responding to it?

Ask your upline leader to listen to you on the phone and provide feedback. Be open to their suggestions.

Get a workout partner and ask them to help you practice your delivery.

Go back to the training. Watch the videos again. Listen and take notes.

Most of all, don't be hard on yourself. You will get better, and so will your results.

2. NOT DOING IT ENOUGH

Many distributors do the right activities and do them the right way, but struggle because they don't do them enough.

They talk to one or two new prospects a week, instead of one or two (or more) a day. They approach a total of five people and when nobody is interested they say the business doesn't work and quit. Or they talk to the same prospects over and over again instead of contacting new ones.

Network marketing is a numbers game. You have to talk to a lot of people to find the ones who are interested. You have to sign up a lot of people to find the ones who will follow the system and become a leader.

If you're doing everything right, but not seeing the results you want, you've got to increase your numbers. Approach more prospects. Do more exposures. Do more 3-way calls.

Some distributors spend too much time checking their stats, posting on social media, and reviewing their notes instead of doing exposures.

Do your exposures first. They are a priority. Take care of administrative tasks after hours, when it's too late to call people.

One way to ensure that you do your daily exposures is to get an *accountability partner*. Find another distributor who also wants to improve their results and agree to hold each other accountable. Share your goals with each other and do a daily check-in to report your activities.

Did you do your exposures today? You either did or you didn't. You'll be more likely to do them when you know someone else is watching.

3. LACK OF BELIEF

By far, the biggest reason distributors struggle is a lack of belief.

They don't believe in the business, the company, the products, their upline or themselves.

If you have doubts, you're not going to be fully committed to the business. You're not going to do the activities, or do them consistently. You'll look for reasons to justify your belief that you're not good enough or the company isn't the right one for you.

If you have doubts, you have to address them. An ounce of doubt and you're out.

The best way to build your belief is to become a prospect again. Go back to square one and sell yourself on the business.

Watch the videos again, go the presentation and watch it as a prospect would, write down your questions and get them answered.

Talk to successful distributors and have them tell you their story (again). Ask them about their doubts and how they overcame them.

Go to the big events—the regionals and conventions—and look at the big picture. Meet the top leaders and get excited all over again.

Whatever you do, don't compare yourself to others. There is no success time-line; it's different for everyone.

If you see someone quickly get to the top of the comp plan, the odds are they have had previous network marketing experience.

They put in several years learning how to recruit and build a team before they joined your company.

Many distributors who struggle have unreasonable expectations about how long it will take to become successful. If you haven't made much money yet, if your team isn't growing the way you thought it would, re-examine your expectations. Most people overestimate what they can do in one year and underestimate what they can do in five years.

You may simply have to give the business more time.

ACTION STEPS/POINTS TO REMEMBER

- If you're not doing the right things in your business, or you're not doing them the right way, you can improve. Get more training, practice, and give it time. You can do this.

- The best way to improve your results is to increase your exposures. Find ways to do that. Talk to distributors who are one or two levels up from where you are. Ask them to share their numbers with you. How many exposures do they do each day? How much time does it take them? What tools and approaches do they use?

- If you or someone on your team is struggling, it might be a lack of belief. Start over and re-sell yourself on the business. Get excited again and then get busy.

DON'T FORGET!

Sign Up For My <u>FREE</u> Recruiting Tips Newsletter and get tips and ideas to help you grow your business:

RecruitAndGrowRich.com/newsletter

ONE LAST THING

If you enjoyed this book, there are two ways you can spread the word:

#1: You Can Write a Review

Reviews of my books are one of the best ways to get the word out. You'll be helping others learn how to work with new distributors, and you'll be helping me. You can share anything, but here are a few ideas:

- What you liked best about the book

- Your favorite chapter or idea

- 3 things you're going to implement from the book

- The results you expect to get or have already received from the book

Go leave a brief a review. Even a few lines helps. If you don't have time to do that, just click and add some stars.

#2 Tell Other Network Marketers You Know

Tell your upline about *Network Marketing Made Simple*. And tell your team. Send an email or text with the title of the book and a link.

Here's the link: http://recruitandgrowrich.com/nmms

I greatly appreciate your support! Please let me know if I can help you with anything.

Thank you!

David M. Ward

ABOUT THE AUTHOR

David M. Ward is an attorney, business owner, marketing consultant, and author.

Ward started in network marketing to build retirement income and to escape the long hours of his law practice. "I was a victim of the self-employment trap—trading my time for dollars," he says. "The bigger my practice grew, the harder I had to work."

After twenty years, he was ready for a change. "Network marketing gave me the time freedom and financial freedom I always wanted."

Ward has been recognized as a six-figure income earner and top recruiter in his network marketing company. He and his wife live in southern California.

recruitandgrowrich.com
recruitingbook@gmail.com